Sex, Pleasure &
Spirituality

By

Kevin Jr. and Shamil Cole

Copyright © 2017

INTRODUCTION

In order to project the positive vibes which are necessary to draw the energies of the universe to you it is essential that you be one hundred percent confidant in your ability to effect a change and willing to believe that all of the events occurring up to that point have been a necessary prerequisite to bringing these events to be. The decision to connect is the core of affection. Daily you're compelled to make connection choices. By your actions you choose what to associate with and what to void. If you wish to grow consciously, you must intentionally choose which connections you'll fortify and which you'll let soften.

Chapter One: Connecting

To connect implies to give something your care, to consider it, and to engage with it. As well as connecting with individuals, you are able to connect with groups, things, places, thoughts, values, and actions. Building a link calls for nothing but your tending. Consider your mom. Consider democracy. Consider your preferred song. Put your attention on something and you at once associate with it. Such principles are rooted in fearfulness and disconnection, and they've no place in a life story of conscious development. When you make the dedication to live consciously, you'll frequently discover yourself battling with the principles. If you want to become more loving, you have to be wishing to connect. In order to discover and grow, you have to be freed to connect with what you wish and to unplug from what you don't wish. No one may provide you that freedom. It's your right as a human. You don't require anybody's permission to choose which associations are most beneficial for you. It's up to you to accept the initiative to associate with what you wish and to unplug from what you don't wish. By consciously arriving at connections that feel intuitively right to you, you direct yourself into the right spot with the rationale of affection. You communicate effectively by firstly associating with the familiar and then broadening into the unfamiliar. When you meet somebody new, the opening move is to find out your shared concerns, values, and mental attitude. This produces a basic adherence of trust and friendship.

The following measure is to research and learn from your differences. Individuals who are too dissimilar from you are hard to bond with, and those who are too like you can't teach you a great deal. The most beneficial relationships supply enough mutual ground to forge a strong bond while as well arousing growth in fresh directions. The deepest form of communicating is common face-to-face conversation. This lets you find out not only content but likewise vocal aspects and body language. You'll commonly experience much richer associations with individuals when you communicate in the flesh rather than by telephone or email. Great communicating skills take time to formulate. The more you rehearse, the better you'll become. While there are particular methods you may learn like smiling, sustaining an open posture, and attaining eye contact, don't forget that the main purpose of communicating is to produce a connection with the other individual. Even when you've a particular agenda in mind such as persuasion, training, or amusement, your opening move is to institute a bond. It isn't adequate to speak your mind and presume others comprehend and accept what you're stating, nor is it adequate to listen well and assume you comprehend what's been stated. To communicate advantageously, there must be some bond between talker and listener. There are few better delights in life than the experience of conscious communicating with another individual. No self-importance games, false fronts, or manipulative maneuvers are utilized. Both people merely wish to connect with one another for the propose of learning and developing.

When you've went through such exposed, loving communicating with another human, it's difficult to go with anything less. Think about your relationship with another individual. Where does it in reality exist? It does not exist anyplace in the outside world. You can't merely point to it and state. "This is our relationship right here." It lives strictly inside your thoughts. Therefore, your association with a different individual is whatever you believe it is. Your notion makes the relationship substantial. If you discontinue to believe in it, then for all pragmatic purposes, it no more exists. The tangible residue might stay on, like a specific living arrangement, but the real human connection will have been left behind. When you comprehend that there's no such thing as an extraneous relationship and that all such associations subsist entirely in your brain, you will become well aware that the real aim of relationships is self exploration. If you communicate in any manner, you're in truth researching different facets of yourself. Once you feel a rich sense of sharing with another individual, you're in reality connecting profoundly with a crucial part of yourself. By sharing with other people, you discover how to love yourself more totally. Each day I get a heavy volume of email feedback through my site. A lot of it comes from individuals who've never encountered me in person, nor have they ever had one conversation with me.

All the same, due to the heavy volume of personal data I've shared on the net, many believe me to be a close friend as they understand so much about me, so they drop a line to me from the position that we already share a bond of affection.

In their very beginning message to me, a lot of individuals will tell me matters about themselves they won't even tell their mates. In their brains, they've already went through such a solid communion with me over a time period of weeks or months that they feel easy talking about their most secret affairs. Naturally I do my best to respect such associations in the loving intent in which they are offered up. From my own inner position, all the same, an even more potent shift has happened. I notice that as I've intensified my own sharing with myself by having a look at my thoughts on paper, my outside world has changed over to reflect that inner growth. Rather than opening with shallow chitchat, individuals start conversations with me by right away plunging into matters of grand importance to them. Even adolescents speak to me in this way. The more I share with myself on the inside, the richer my relationships with other people get to be. Nowadays, my life story brims over with opportunities for sound human association. For a long time, I've witnessed abundant evidence that our relationships with other individuals always reverberate our inner relationships with assorted parts of ourselves. If you've trouble connecting with individuals on the exterior, it might be because you aren't sharing with yourself on the interior. Once you discover how to feel fondly connected on the interior, you'll discover it much simpler to form a bond with other people. All humans are created with the natural need to give and receive affection.

We're created in love which forms the basis of our divine spiritual selves, and of our physically manifested life. Even the many limits that we encounter in our early lives don't remove affection from our spiritual center, because it's the essence of who we are. When you relinquish control in your life and relationships and have faith, you open a space in your life for something fresh to come in and let yourself release the stress. You're accepting what is and adjusting your energies and efforts towards other more positive actions. Cut down stress and anxiety by utilizing the following steps to relinquish control in your life. There are so a lot of situations where you just wish to hang on to a particular way of believing, acting or doing things as you don't wish to be proven "wrong". Take a rich breath and relinquish the need to be correct. If you're attempting to control somebody else's behavior, realize that it isn't healthy for you or for that individual. Take a piece of paper and put down all your expectations of that individual and then rip up that sheet of paper and let them go. Quit fighting or resisting what is and alter your need to command the situation so that you are able to have some peace and recover that energy that you've been using up in an unfruitful place. Acknowledging that you're "incorrect" for hanging on in some instances may actually be very "right" for your life. Occasionally just the cognizance that you're hanging on to control isn't enough. If you keep hanging on to control and use up unbelievable amounts of energy balking change, then sit down and work out precisely why.

Take out your journal and put down the top 3 things that you'll let go of when you relinquish control. Do you fear that if you let go, you'll lose a relationship? Do you feel that if you alter your life-style, you'll lose your comfort zone? Are you nervous and stressed out at the thought of having change? Believe. If you don't have faith, you can't trust. But he is there. Stay centered on your faith. It will help you to stay grounded, and not center on all the abominable things going on around you. Believe in the higher powers abilities. If we really believe in all of the higher powers abilities and mights, we'll never be afraid or worried that something won't work out. It stretches our own faith and belief, when we go through hard times. Believe in the higher powers willingness to help you through the hard time. He doesn't want you to quell in the bad time; he wants you to learn some lesson from it. Ask him what the lesson is, and to assist you through it. Believe the higher power can and will work matters out for good. Things are always the hardest when we can't see the other side of our worries. We can't determine how it will work out. This truly stretches our faith as all we can see are the hard conditions in front of us. Trusting the higher power seems exceedingly difficult. The higher power is calling us to believe what seems inconceivable. Ask him to help you trust. Remember the great things the higher power has done in the past. The great things the higher power has previously done remind us that he may still do good things once more. If the higher power provided revenue for you in the past, be assured he may provide revenue for you again. If the higher power did something unbelievable for you at one time, he can do it again.

Chapter Two: Positive Expression

If you're tempted to fret, put a different, better thought in your head. Keep doing this each time the concern returns. This is the only way to quit worrying. You have to replace the distressing thoughts with something more beneficial. Many experiments reveal that sex is the main factor between relationship and fun. Couples make fun with this process. Sexuality is not a positive expression, though it is considered as a negative sight in many societies. Sex enables to tie the long term relationship and it is the key of successful relationship. It is seen that many of us neglect sex because of insufficient knowledge onit. Sex is one of the vital causes of long term enjoyment. If you think that sex is only a physical event, then you will not understand the main theme of it. It is not only a physical event but also a spiritual event. One can attain amusement and satisfaction quite easily after having sex with his or her partner. It is mandatory to give priority to your partner's satisfaction. If you can ensure it, then you and your partner will certainly enjoy this special event. Sex has thepower of tranquility. It is the fact here and that's why you must follow these guidelines. We often hear that sex is placed against religion, but it is not true. The Bible gives a special place to sex. We can easily understand the fact from the love poem of the Bible named "The Song of Solomon". It shows the positive potentials of having sex with your marriage partner. Actually, sex is the media of creating intimacy between and husband and wife.

It helps in gaining marital maturity. Fragrance, intimate talking, privacy, commitment and affectionate touching can easily make your event unique and that is why you must maintain them while you are havingsex with your life partner. Commitment is the main factor to totally enjoy sex. We can say that sex enables an individual to love and sacrifice. That's why sexuality is often compared with spirituality. Moreover, sex helps to produce strong bonding and close relationship. Today, people are very busy and have no time to consider this. That's why many families are breaking regularly. You must pay attention to the sexual requirement of your life partner. Both physical and emotional requirements should be fulfilled. In ancient times, sex was an event to meet one's physical needs but that has changed over time. It is not only confined in physical satisfaction, but also needs mental satisfaction.Sex is really a special event in any couple's life. Couples try their best to satisfy each other during this special time. Sex and sexuality is closely related with spirituality. In the ancient times, people had sex only to satisfy their physical needs, but this has changed over time. Now people need both physical and mental satisfaction. Sex is the means of enjoyment and that's why it has a special attraction to both men and women. Many people still consider this special event as a sin, but it is true that sex is always given a special place in all religions. The Bible has placed sex as an important aspect of our life. "The Song of Solomon" expresses the importance and necessities of sex.

Actually,sex is a part and parcel of every couple's life, because it ties the relationship and creates a bond between the couples. That's why sex is a special moment in every person's life. Spiritual sex is the way to show love to your partner. It is the media by which you can show gratitude to your God. It is the fact andthat's why people intend to have spiritual sex now. We have found that most of the sexual moments have lost appeal or enjoyment, because of men's brutality. Men often try to force their partners into having hard sex, but they usually take less time to understand their partners. Spiritual sex enables an individual to understand the feelings of his partner; that means what she actually want from a man. Rape and sexual harassment are both detrimental, because they destroy the morality of an individual. That'swhy they just can't show proper honor to each other. Improper sex may irritate your partner. Men should hide their animal nature, because it can only cause damage to the marital life. Imbalanced sex enables abnormal lifestyle and is harmful toa couple.If you want to enjoy your special moments with your life partner for a long time without any sort of hassles, then you have no other choice than spiritual sex. You must keep this in your mind. There are many men out there who don't care much about a woman's pleasure or how she feels or what she's thinking during sex. Since you're taking the time to read this special report, you are probably not one of those men. And, that's a good start!

You're already a step ahead of most men because you're at least interested in learning more, and maybe becoming better. When men think about "sex secrets," they tend to focus mainly on techniques. They are always trying to learn some new trick or maneuver that will make a woman have wild, screaming orgasms in bed...every single time. And, while that's all fine and good, it's not new "techniques" or tricks that women wish you were focusing on. Women think very differently from men. And, it's what she's thinking about during sex that you should be most concerned about. Of course, the average woman would never tell her (male) lover what she's thinking about let alone what she wishes you knew or did, during sex. It's also important how you say the above phrases. You wouldn't want to come across as someone who has never seen a naked woman before. And, you definitely wouldn't want to sound fake. Also... don't wait for (nor expect) her to respond to your positive comment by saying anything. If she says "thank you" or just smiles, that's great. But, don't wait for it. Awkward silences are not good here. After you tell her how amazing she looks, smile if she's already looking at you, and then kiss her - either on the lips or on her body. Or simply continue doing what you were going to do anyway. Keep things moving. Obviously, this stuff is even more important if the woman does not have a supermodel's body. (And, most women won't.) Women tend to be self-conscious, especially when they're naked, because they don't realize that most guys are just glad that they got naked for you, and are willing to have sex with you.

So, you need to let it be known, or remind her, that she is the most important and the most beautiful woman on the planet right now.. and that all of your focus and attention is on her. Building on the previous section, making her feel comfortable and more confident about what she's doing can even help her to do more - and new - things for you. (That can be very good for you.) The truth is, many women want to feel completely uninhibited in bed. They want to go a little wild. and they want to occasionally take control. They want to take charge and try out a new position that they've just read about, and so on. Unfortunately, most times she's either too shy, self-conscious, or embarrassed to do it... or she simply doesn't want to come across as "too experienced," promiscuous, or dog forbid, even slutty. (You can thank society for that one.) It could even be something as simple as "talking dirty" to and with you. But, she may never bring it up herself - even if she's secretly fantasizing about doing it. The way to loosen her up is to increase her overall comfort level. Remember, she has to feel comfortable, relaxed, even lusted after, before she will open up and start doing all the things that she really wants to do with you... including all the things that you really want her to do for you. You can start by making her feel comfortable, safe, and more confident about what she's already doing to/with you...as explained in the earlier section. And, keep letting her know how great she looks... how much her scent/smell, taste, body, moans, etc. is turning you on... Finally, pay attention!

Here's a few tips for men, juct in case your wondering how to wow the socks off a woman. You probably have a woman in mind that you want to woo or maybe you don't and you just bump into a woman and you were instantly attracted to her , the first thing you would want to do is to have a conversation with her. I have noticed that most men find it difficult to approach a woman and initiate conversations with them. Initiating conversation with a woman is a big challenge for most men, some are unsure of how to do this in a respectful manner without sounding rude to the woman; some can hold their own once the ball starts rolling; some cannot converse with a woman at all because they are too shy or timid while some find it hard to communicate at a casual level with other people (men and women inclusive) but   feel very comfortable talking about topics such as football, politics, science, religion etc. The most important thing to keep in mind when approaching a woman   is that first impressions are priceless and are established within the first three seconds after you introduce yourself. This means that there is no room for error and you should also know that chatting up a lady is not like in the movies where you can just walk up to a girl and drop some cheesy one liner: then they are in your bed the next morning. Don't use pickup lines because they make the lady feel cheap and it destroys conversation. It's hard to think of what to say afterward. Instead, start with innocent small talk, and you will have a base to build an interesting conversation on.

A trick that never fails to work, is to focus all your attention and energy of the creature before you and behave as if nothing else exists in the world. Focus on what the woman needs and not what you need. For instance women are a creature of drama, and will prefer a soap opera to a sport game. Women sense and are turned off by insecurity, so make sure you look and act confident. Groom, dress, move, and pursue like a man who is secure with women and with himself. Be yourself don't fake it. Start by first talking and later making friends with the person you think is special. Most people don't like to jump straight into a relationship, especially girls. Find a reason to talk to the person. Make sure that they want to talk to you. Just talk about something that keeps the conversation going. Be yourself and don't lie just to get to a special person's heart. If they find out later and you're in the middle of a deep relationship or maybe a time when you really need that person, they will leave for good. Let the person know that you like them. Beyond the cheesy sending a note through a friend, talk to them about something you both have in common. If you are meeting the woman for the first time strike a conversation with her and let her know that you admire her and would want to know her better, introduce yourself and ask her for her name and number, if she is interested in you she would ask for your number, if she doesn't don't despair she might be the shy type or the type that believes it is a man's duty to do the chasing.

Tell her that you would call her but don't tell when. Make sure you call her as promised her and ask her for a date. If after the first date two dates what you expected was not what you got or you find out she is not the kind of woman you would want to have a permanent relationship with. Let her know that you could just be friends or break it off don't toy with her feelings. Because if you go on a date with a woman more than twice, she concludes that you are having a permanent relationship with her. If you have known her for long, maybe you have been friends for sometime and you just realize that you want more than friendship, let her know the level you want your friendship to get to. Don't nurse your feelings for her in secret or assume that she wants the same thing. She might be romantically involved with somebody already or she might not want more than friendship with you. Probably she wants you too but does not want to cross the boundary of friendship. Talk with her, tell her how you feel. Act fast before someone beats you to it. Wooing a woman takes planning and strategies as you have known. But planning and strategy has to be within your means. You don't have to break a bank because you want to woo a woman. If she expects you to break a bank before you can get her or make her happy then she is not worth your time, effort and money. There are many good women out there. Leave her. It actually takes little things applied correctly to make most good women happy. Follow these strategies and you would never go wrong.

Chapter Three: Pampering

Going out on dates is actually a must in every relationship, whether you have been married for fifty years or just starting. Our focus is really on the man that has just met a woman he is interested in and a man that has just indicated his interest in a woman he has known for some time. Though, a married man can still use any or all of these ideas to woo his wife because the wooing never really stops. When planning a date, men often think that there are certain things that they should and should not do. Women are individuals, though, and what turns one woman on may be very off-putting and aversive to another. By following a few simple guidelines, you can make sure that the wooing goes smoothly and happily for both of you. A word of warning; if you are on a budget, decide on how much you want to spend and stick to it. Decide on an affordable activity and location, decide on affordable place to dine out or you can as well have a picnic in the middle of your living room, with a nice bottle of wine, candles and the music of your choice can even do the trick if you play the game well. Take her on a planned date, to dinner at a place where she has mentioned that she likes or on a surprise date to a good place you have tried and you think she would like. You can invite her over to your place for dinner or Sunday brunch; make it special by preparing something you think she would like or something she has mentioned that she likes. Take her to watch movies, if she likes movies. If she likes sports you can go and watch a sporting event together.

Take her to the Olympics, just kidding; you can go on a drive together to a predetermined spot. Serenade her sometimes by singing a love song outside her window. Go to a coffee house and read poetry to each other. Call your local radio station and make a request for her favorite song or any love song to be played and make sure she is listening, by first sending a text message to her asking her to listen to the particular radio station at the said time. Enjoy the outdoors; picnic in your local park or at your local beach; host a candlelight dinner in your own backyard, patio or terrace, use the stars as your backdrop and candles to create intimacy. You can watch the sun go down or the moon come up together. You can also visit the Museum or National Park together It is exciting to try new things, but don't go too far outside of either of your comfort zones. It doesn't really matter how much money you spend, or how gallant you are. In the end, it's a man's sensitivity and compatibility which really impresses a woman. Giving gifts is a good way of showing your woman that you appreciate her, because that is what she really wants from you. When buying her gifts put some thought to it, don't only give her gifts on her birthdays, Valentine's Day and on other known holidays. Surprise her with a gift from time to time. Buy her things that she likes, it might just be something she mentioned that she likes during the course of your conversation. Something you feel would make her smile.

It is not the cost of the gift that matters to her but the fact that you thought of her and that made you to buy something for her. It can be something as simple as her favourite flower, candy, chocolates, bath goodies or pricey gifts like jewelleries. Something you are able to afford. Take the time to wrap the gift, and get a card. This seems silly; of course a gift is just as good if it isn't wrapped. However, giving a wrapped gift and a sentimental card will make her feel even more like a queen to you. You can even give her pampering gifts like manicure/pedicure gift certificate or massage products or give certificates. Let her know you are thinking of her give her something special not generic. This is a very important tool in a relationship make out time to communicate with her, call her when you promise to call, call her when she does not expect you to call, send her romantic text messages and if you are a good writer, write romantic poems. Be attentive, listen to her don't always do the talking learn to listen to her. Make the effort to sit down across from her after a long day to discuss work, friends and your relationship. Don't force the topic toward the relationship. Concentrate on her, do not only look at her focus on her: her eyes, her body language and her voice, let her know that she has your undivided attention. Notice when she is happy and when she is sad try to make her happy. Let her know at all times that you care her. Communication is how we get to know each other. The ability to listen is a great tool, and in case you're wondering, no, it's not the same thing as hearing.

If you're out on a date and getting your lady to open up is like pulling teeth, ask her about her interests and things you know she's passionate about. She might just need that little push to get going, and if talking about her passion for photography is what does the trick, just make sure you're all ears. By being an attentive listener, it'll encourage her to open up and chat away, and she'll gain your trust. And if you prove that you're listening, getting her to be quiet might become your next problem. A little bit of generosity goes a long way. This doesn't necessarily mean monetary generosity. Perhaps your woman has been having financial problems, or perhaps she's been having difficulty with a relative or her boss. If you lend a compassionate ear, she will come away with a good impression of you and the date you had together. Listening is a skill many men have difficulty with, but it is one of the most important skills any man can possess. If her openness makes you feel uncomfortable, just nod and smile. Try to find areas where you have something in common. Be considerate; always show kindness and courteousness towards her. Open the car door for her, offer to drive her (and drive safely, so as not to frighten her). Always pay for the first date. Be punctual when picking her up. Be kind to waiters and cab drivers Women appreciate a man who is respectful, as it says a lot about how he will treat her and whether or not he respects women in general.

Some people find this practice outdated. Be awesome at anything; if you are smart, show it off, if you are funny, make her laugh, or if you are good at sports, give a demonstration. Let her know how you are different. Pay attention to positive traits, features and character about her. It does not have to be complex, it may even be simply letting her know that you love the way she is dressed or her hair is styled. Tell her things like "You have such beautiful smile" State your compliments by looking her straight in the eye this emphasizes the sincerity of your compliments. Body compliments should be avoided in the initial stage of your interaction but compliment do compliment on her later and always in the relationship. Compliment her on her brains, jokes and talents and be very sincere in your compliments.Never compromise your morals. If the person you are interested in is not interested in you, then you should move on. Some people are very polite and you may not realize immediately that they aren't interested. But, given time, it should become apparent. In the meantime, take it slow, and even if you are head over heels, don't reveal this right away, at least until you are sure they are genuinely interested in you, too, or they could use your attraction to their benefit. Usually it is best to reveal one's feelings step by step, not much more nor much less than the other has revealed. However, people have very different ways for showing that they are or are not interested, so do not break up, or step it up, without talking things through as to where you're both headed. If you feel like you need time to decide, do not hesitate to talk.

Never be forceful. If you ever pressure her to do something she doesn't feel comfortable doing, she won't be shy to say goodbye. Forcing her to do what she doesn't want to do is rude. Try to continue doing your normal routine, with them in mind, rather than changing your whole life around them. Hopefully they will want to have a relationship with you, not a clone of themselves or a tag along. The most important thing in dating is to be conscious of your date's feelings and reactions. If she's a high-powered lawyer or a free-thinking intellectual, she may feel that your chivalry is an attempt to deprive her of her independence. However, if she's pleased at your holding the door for her, keep up the gallantry. A lot of guys choose women who are "arm candy" good-looking trophy girlfriends who bolster their status among other men or counteract their own insecurities. That's all well and good, but if you find a woman who makes you happy, regardless of looks, age or social status or what any other guy thinks then you have definitely won at the mating game. Satisfaction is very important for sex. There are physical satisfaction and mental satisfaction. Both are necessary. Many experiments have revealed that sex is the key factor between long term relationship and fun. Couples make fun during sex. Sexuality is not a negative expression, though it is considered negative in many societies. It helps maintain long term relationship and it is the key of any successful relationship. If you think that sex is only a physical event, then you will not understand its main theme.

Chapter Four: Good Sex

It is not only a physical event but also a spiritual event. One can attain amusement and satisfaction quite easily after having sex with his or her partner. It is mandatory to give priority to your partner's satisfaction. If you can ensure that, then you and your partner will certainly enjoy this special event. Sex has a power of tranquility. It is the fact here and that's why you must follow these guidelines. You have to try to understand the needs of your partner while you are having sex with him or her. Sex is a means of enjoyment. It helps remove depression and enhances happiness. It is the fact that has been revealed by several experiments. There are many other advantages of having sex. Proper sex can easily solve the problem of fertility. Moreover, good sex is one of the main factors of a happy life. We see that many of us still believe that sex is a sin and that's why wefeel shameful and guilty to share the sexual contents with others. But it is true that sex is not a sin and it is one of the beautiful gifts of God to us. When you try to satisfy your life partner, is it the way to satisfy God? We have found that the Bible has kept a special place for sex and knowledge of sex helps you to understand the fact. Sex and sexuality have a close connection with spirituality. Both men and womenare greatly attracted to sex, though their sexuality differs. Sexual satisfaction is the aim of sex. If you just think that it is only a physical need, then your ideology needs modification. It is not only a physical demand, but also a mental demand. Good sex has the ability to satisfy an individual both mentally and physically.

You have to change your outlook first. Rape or sexual harassment should be avoided, because these can destroy the morality of an individual. Sex with commitment can tie the bonding of a relationship. It is the main cause of long term relationship. Today,we see that people are very busy in outdoor work and they have no time to spend with theirlife partners. Commitment between husband and wife ensures good sex which thenensures long term relationship. People should give much priority on this factor. Actually,sex is a biological and psychological need. One can enjoy a happy moment easily, if he gives priority on the mindset. Proper planning is essential for good sex. It is often seen that a man tries to dominate the woman in bed which is very bad. You have to change your mentality and try to understand what your partner expects from you. If your partner is not satisfied with your behavior, then how can you expect to enjoysex with her in thebed? There are several ways to satisfy each other in the bed. Massages, changing positions, emotional talking, good commitment etc. are the preconditions of good and enjoyable sex. It is true that people often neglect these during the physical climaxes and that's why they fail to enjoy sex. Sex is one of the most popular means of enjoyment. One can easily get both physical and emotional satisfaction from it. Any sort of mistake in this special moment can destroy the whole moment. A good sex is mandatory for a married couple. It ties the bond and helps to understand each other. That's why you have to set your mind first to enjoy the spiritual satisfaction of sex.

The benefits of mindset for sexual satisfaction are many. One must set his mind before going to have sex with his girlfriend. Generally,women show less eagerness to sex than men and that's why your first job is to create the sexual appeal toyour partner. You need to raise consciousness of your partner too. If you fail to raise sexual appeal of your partner, then it is recommended by the experts to talk with her for a while. You must avoid over reacting, because it can hamper your personality in front of your partner. In some cases, we see that people get nervous while they have sex. Some men feel that they need to act differently while having sex, which shouldn't be assex is quite a normal thing. Instead, if someone progress from one step to the next smoothly, there is every chance to make that sexual work build a nice and pleasant impression on the mindset of one's partner. Nothing should be done hurriedly. Sloth in sex will make it more enjoyable and satisfactory. Another way to boost the mindset is to avoid negative thinking. Generally,we see that we unnecessarily think about the future leaving the present. While walking to our workplace, we think of what's goingon at the officeand during sex about the duration of ejaculation –whether it is too fast or not, whether the duration could have satisfied the partner or not, etc. Such sort of negative thinking makes us stressed and prevents us from enjoying the game. We should relax and stay in present during sex to reach the utmost level of satisfaction. We have to concentrate on the present condition and should have sex for long time with detailed physical activities to make it more enjoyable.

The art of touch has a great importance during sex. Women love to be touched. If a man can touch her smoothly and softly, it will surely ensure his success in seducing her. Touching has a taming power and creates a positive effect on women's mind thathelpsstimulate their sexual appetite. This is a prerequisite for an enjoyable sex. So, men must spend sometime in touching their women to drive them crazy for having sex. If someone is not hungry, food will not turn up to be tasteful to him. Likewise, if someone's sex appetite is not aroused, sex will not be enjoyable to him/her. As in the case of attraction, stereotype conception plays the vital role, so does attraction in a relationship.It is natural forhuman beings to feel attracted to the opposite sex. Some people think that it's only the men who are attracted to women while the women are not. This is a fully wrong conception. Both the male and the female feel attractedtowards their opposite sex. But the mode of expression varies. Men are straight in expressing their attraction to women whereas women turn up to be just the opposite. To build up a good relationship, attraction from the sides isessential. Boththe female and the maleshould be attracted tooneanother. It's the prerequisite of a relation. The criteria of attraction are variable. They vary from person to person according to their choices. No two individuals are alike. It is also true in regards of their taste on which the choice of partner basically depends. The feelings of attraction drive us to a nice relation and the more intense the attraction is, the deeper the relationship grows.

So, to make a relationship, one must have to become able to attract his/her desired person. A person's feelings of attraction basically depend on what he/she likes. So, to attract someone towards oneself,one has to do according to the likings of one's desired person. As time passes by, attraction becomes intense. Human mind is such a thing that once it gets stuck to something, it can't leave or move from that to the other. Likewise, once a person appears to be attractive to someone, the attraction increases as time passes by So, the first impression is the most important factor to others. Likewise, a sweet and harmonic relationship is a prerequisite for a satisfactory relationship. The more the partners are attracted to each other, the more they get satisfied with each other. Attraction is also a sexual stimulator since sex plays a vital role in the development and continuation of arelationship. Satisfaction ina relationship also includes sexual satisfaction andmental satisfaction. Here,we see the deep inter-relation between these terms. None of them can be thought about by leaving another. Each of them is related to each other. As we know, love is the best doctor, so we can say that mental satisfaction is impossible without love and love doesn't happen without the feelings of attraction. This is the universal law of attraction and satisfaction. Sex is one of the great means of pleasure for both man and woman. People search tranquilityand enjoyment with this activity. God has created sex inthe universe and we enjoy it as his blessing. Actually,it is a gift from God to us.

.

In the ancient times, people had sex only to satisfy their physical needs, but time has been changed a lot. Now, people need both physical and mental satisfaction. Sex is the means of enjoyment and that's why both men and women are attracted to it. It is true that sexuality and spirituality are closely related. Spirituality is the way to remove the misconception of having sex. Today most of the relationships are breaking without any proper reason. It is just enough to describe the bonding between husbandand wife. Separations are always negative and it creates frustration in an individual's life. Sex is the only wayto eradicate this sort of frustration. Sex means being closed or connected and that's why the term "spirituality" comes. Partners try heart and soul to satisfy each other. Spiritual sex helps an individual to lead a happy and enjoyable life. Actually,sex is an art and it is one of the vital weapons of any relationship. Many experiments have revealed that sex is the main factor between relationship and fun. Couples make fun with this process. Sexuality is not a positive expression, though it is considered as negative in many societies. It enables to tie the long term relationship and it is the key of successful relationship. It is seen that many of us neglect sex because of insufficient knowledge about it. Sex is one of the vital causes of long term enjoyment. If you think that sex is only a physical event, then you will not understand the main theme of it. It is not only a physical event but also a spiritual event. One can attain amusement and satisfaction quite easily after having sex with his or her partner.

It is mandatory to give priority to your partner's satisfaction. If you can ensure it, then you and your partner will certainly enjoy this special event.Sex has the power of tranquility. It is the fact here and that's why you must follow these guidelines. Sexually satisfied people lead a happy life than any other people. Sex and satisfaction are interrelated and people have sex for satisfaction. We all know that satisfaction is mainly of two types. The first one is physical satisfaction and the other is mental or emotional satisfaction. When you are going to have sex with your life partner, you probably seek both from her. Isn't it? Actually,sex without emotional satisfaction is nothing. In the ancient times, people had sex only to satisfy theirphysical needs, but time it haschangedover time. Now people need both physical and mental satisfaction. Sex is the means of enjoyment and that's whyboth men and womenare strongly attracted to it. It is true that sexuality and spirituality are closely related. Spirituality is the way to remove the misconception of having sex. Today,most of the relationships are breaking without any proper reason. It is just enough to describe the bonding between husband and wife. Separations arealways negative and it creates frustration in an individual's life. Sex is the only way to eradicate this sort of frustration. Sex means being closed or connected and that's why the term "spirituality" comes. Partners try heart and soul to satisfy each other. Spiritual sex helps an individual to lead a happy and enjoyable life. That's why spiritual sex is the way to express your love to your partner.

It is usually seen that most of the sexual moments have lost appeal or enjoyment, because of brutality and sick mentality of men. Men often try to force his partners to have hard sex, but they usually takeless time to understand their wives. Spiritual sex enables an individual to understand the feelings of his partner; that means what she wants actually from a man. Rape and sexual harassment are both detrimental, because theydestroy the morality of an individual. That's why they just can't show proper honor to each other. Improper sex is responsible for irritating behavior of an individual. Men must hide their animal nature, because it can cause only damage to the marital life. Imbalanced sex enables abnormal lifestyle and is harmful for a couple. If you want to enjoy your special moments with your life partner for a long time without any sort of hassles, then you have no other choice than spiritual sex. You must keep these in your mind. Satisfaction is a relative idea and you just can't measure it. It is not possible to measure the quantity of satisfaction, but quality can be measured. A good understanding is necessary for the couple to enjoy their sexual time. A good commitment is also essential. If you think that sex is only a physical event, then you will not understand the main theme of it. It is not only a physical event but also a spiritual event. One can attain amusement and satisfaction quite easily after having sex with his or her partner. It is mandatory to give priority to your partner's satisfaction.

Chapter Five: Energy And Strive

If you can ensure it, then you and your partner will certainly enjoy this special event. In a recent experiment on sexual happiness, it has been revealed that some sort of additional tasks before sex like massages, commitment, emotional talking, altering positions etc. can be helpful in enjoying this beautiful moment. For the more discerning few, the exercise of finding one's life purpose is anything but frivolous. Finding one's purpose in life will help to give the individual a real picture of either his or her capabilities and put these into action to achieve the purpose perceived. It gives the individual the zest for life instead of just simply existing day to day on mundane and often exhausting and stressful regimens. Identifying the purpose of one's existence also allow the individual to enjoy a certain level of fulfillment and peace as the energy used to strive towards the end goal becomes well worth the effort. It also provides the individual with a concept to live by and the positive energy will help the individual through thick and thin. People who are able to find their purpose are usually people on a mission to get the most out of their lives, and they are also usually very driven, focused and energized. Keeping healthy both mentally and physically are the common traits of those who seem to have identified their purpose in life. In order to get the promotion you are dreaming about the first thing you must do is remove any doubt from your mind. Walk into the interview one hundred percent sure that the position will be yours; remember, if you are still living with the belief that the position may be above you and you are not certain that you have the necessary skills to fill the position you are absolutely right.

This causes the individual to lose any passion felt as the job does not in any way stimulate the mind and body to give the best possible results it can. Being stuck in the seemingly endless cycle does not encourage the individual to look to the future with anticipation and excitement. Therefore to get the best out of life itself, the individual would be required to spend some time and effort to actually explore the possibility of understanding his or her true calling and working on fulfilling this call. The positive outcome of being able to understand the true calling has far reaching effects on the individual's life in general. Everything will seem better and clearer and the individual will eventually be able to find happiness in the most simple of things. Reaching this level of mental and physical connection is something most people are never able to enjoy through their lifetime, due to their inability to make concerted efforts to understand the true calling of their existence. Being able to deal positively and honestly with the feelings and thoughts will help the individual better identify the inner voice that is so in tune with the true calling meant for him or her. Taking the time to stop and think really hard about what really excites, stimulates and interests them will help to narrow down the quest to finding the true calling they were designed to embark upon. Intuition is usually closely connected to or associated with women, as men are perceived to be rather too "shallow" both in body and mind to be able to tap into or feel such depth the intuitions normally dictates.

Feeling something without actually knowing the source of the prompting could be categorized as intuition and when an individual chooses to ignore such promptings, there are usually dire consequences to be paid. A lot of people especially women rely heavily on the particular style of seeking and getting answers or solutions to a situation or problems that is weighing heavily on their mind. A more complex and scientifically acknowledged form would be the multisensory perception whereby the individual would claim to experience a hunch or an acute prompting about a particular element. This is a very sophisticated system that connects, with elements within and outside the human body and mind to produce enlightening perceptions in general. With practice this exercise can be called upon and interpreted accordingly, while still acknowledging that is does require some extensive understanding which unless the individual is tuned into will not bring forth the desired results. Being able to practice being intuitive will certainly help when wanting to explore life's challenges and directions for the individual. It is essential that once you have placed a request for a significant other with the universe that you be willing to have patience for the desired results to occur. The whys and wherefores of this will be discussed in more depth a bit later, but for now let us look at the obvious. The universe is not always going to give you exactly what you want, exactly when you want it. It does things in its own time.

Now, imagine that you have asked the universe to give you the man or woman of your dreams, but you become impatient because they have not yet become a part of your life within a few months of making the request. You begin to date someone else, and that someone else begins to occupy your mind and your attentions until they are all that you see. They are not the person which you asked the universe for, however; they are simply someone intended to fill the time until that person arrives. Over the course of time that you are dating this other individual, however, you have become acquainted with quite a lot of new people. These new people are shadows passing in and out of your life because they are not this new person whom you have begun to date. What would you do if the person you had been waiting for was among that number? What if they had come looking for you, but you did not recognize them because you were so busy trying to keep yourself busy until they got there? It is essential that you not close either your mind or your heart to the universe because of external distractions; this is the most fatal mistake you could make, for it means that you have lost faith in the ability of the energies of your mind to interact with the energies of nature to bring you your desired results, and the negative energies generated from these thoughts will result in the person of your dreams walking away from you before you even knew they were there.

As you will have gathered from previous sections, the law of attraction does not always work the way that all parties involved would like it to. Why is that? After all, in the law of attraction is universal, why does it only work part of the time? The answer to that is found in the minds of the people who are attempting to use it to their own benefit. The only thing standing between you and success is yourself; this was discussed earlier. If the mind is clogged with so much negative energy that it cannot release the positive vibes which will attract the positive energies of the universe, the law of attraction will not be able to help them. They must first rid themselves of all of these negative vibes and start fresh. As with any skill it takes time, effort and devotion to truly master the use of the law of attraction in your life. There are a number of factors which can cause the law to behave in ways which you may not have expected, almost all of which fall back on the user's ability to follow the guidelines required to find success with this fabulous new tool. Fortunately, the mistakes which are made with regards to the use of the law of attraction are as universal as it is, and therefore very easy to identify and correct. Believing that positive thinking is enough to attract what you want. Positive thinking occurs only on the conscious level; this is why positive thinking is not enough to put into effect the law of attraction. It is necessary for belief to enter the subconscious as well.

The mind is always operating on two levels, the subconscious and the conscious. The conscious mind is being given hundreds of tidbits of information at any given time from all five senses. This is an incredible amount of information to process, even from such an advanced tool as the human brain. The mind would slowly go crazy if it had to deal with all of that information all of the time. Instead, the mind developed the conscious mind, which serves as a filter to review the information sent to it by the senses and retain anything that it deems important. Anything that it does not deem important is passed along to the subconscious. It is the subconscious which will retain this information, acting as the guardian of repressed memories until such time as those memories are needed again. It has long been held that the subconscious has a direct effect on the actions and beliefs of the conscious mind, a topic which will be discussed in greater detail a bit later on, but for now it is sufficient to say that if the conscious mind is attempting to think positive thoughts. Most people have a few core values they live by and understand the extent they are willing to go to ensure these core values are not compromised in any way, will show the inner character of the individual. Some of these core values may include elements of honesty, hardworking styles, perseverance and many other actions or characteristics that define the individual. These values are the elements that usually carry the individual through tough situations, where decisions made are based on these values.

Priorities are usually given to this mindset and judgment calls are made in line with this, thus it is important to be able to fall back on some really good and strong value systems. The important question that should be the focus of the individual's life, would be if he or she was living life according to these values or if there were numerous compromised being made, in order to be pleasing or accommodating to others. If the individual finds that compromise seems to be the general agenda in their lives, the outcome will eventually cause the individual to perhaps become a negative person, as frustration takes hold and values are abandoned. Therefore besides the exercise of exploring the value system the individual perceives to adhere to, it is perhaps more important to ensure these values are completely understood and practiced on a daily basis. This is what eventually defines the individual as different and help make it possible to happily acknowledge that they value their beliefs greatly. Knowing that one is living according to a value system that is part of the mind and body will definitely bring about a deep sense of satisfaction. There is a lot of misguided acceptance that an individual will eventually control and influence the mind and body to learn to accept circumstances and make the best of them. This may be true to a certain extent but it will not really help the individual to bring out the talents that may be hidden deep within. Most times these talents are not used simply because the individual is really unaware of its existence, thus making it impossible to capitalize on them.

Then there is also the thought process that encourages people to strive for being the very best in whatever endeavor they decide to take on. Any success is then related and connected to the perceived talent it took to bring the endeavor to its current success state. This too is not really the inner talent that is so popularity talked about. Life in general is confusing enough, without the added confusion of having the figure out who we really are and our purpose. Most people try and define who they are, using the ever common method by linking their lives to what they do, but this does not really define the person. When questioned, most people respond according to what they do rather than really know who they are in terms of purpose in life. The idea is to be able to differentiate between the two and really explore the possibilities through finding one's purpose in life, and one way of doing this would be to turn to the art of numerology. The idea of using numerology can seem to be confusing and a rather skeptical one, but by simply using facts such as the name and date of birth, an individual is able to gain some insight into the realm of finding the life's purpose. Some sources believe that numerology does help to steer an individual according to the path of life mapped out by connecting factors that may be beyond comprehension. Numerology is sometimes considered an ancient occult that helps an individual to find the direction in the life through a series of numbers and their connecting meanings which the life purpose reflects. The two types of numerology would be Chaldean and Pythagorean and these are supposed to help unlock the life directions as seemingly as a manual would.

Using the life purpose number which is basically calculated on the letters of the name, the individual would be able to learn the purpose of life based on the personality traits that might help to send the individual in a certain direction. Many people fail to live purposeful lives simply because they are not really in tune with their mind and body, and are nor focused in exploring the things that most ignite their passions. Getting caught up with the everyday challenges seem to force and individual to put their own personal needs and desires on hold and focus instead on just getting through life's challenges. It is true that you can't attain 100% satisfaction when you are having sex withyour partner. But if you follow some rules, then you will successfully enjoy your special moment with your partner. These tips are given below. Try to understand and respect your partner's emotion. Don't do anything which is against your partner. Avoid over reacting. It is found that proper planning is needed before having sex. Be positive. Commitment is one of the key factors for healthy sex. That's why you must be careful! Some studies have revealed that alcoholic husbands can't satisfy their wives during the time of physical climaxes. Moreover, they often neglect emotional satisfaction. Marital conflict is one of the major causes of sexual dissatisfaction. Those who violate commitment can never enjoy this special moment. Those who avoid emotional talking before sex are found to be dissatisfied sexually.

Dominating behavior is also responsible for dissatisfaction in sex. It is usually found that most of the men have this irresponsible behavior and that's why it sucks. Any sort of brutality or harassment can destroy your special moment. A good commitment helps in sexual satisfaction. Emotional talking before sex helps couple enjoytheir special time. Position changing has a great impact. Give priority to your partner's demand. Try to understand her feelings. Long time sex with slow process can be helpful in this sort of condition. We can say that sex is not a sin. It is one of the precious gifts from God. That's why we have to give priority to our life partner in order to have sexual satisfaction. Now turn your attention to your anticipations. Where do you truthfully see your present relationships going? Which ones are developing, and which are drifting away? Where is your momentum taking you? What does your current situation tell you about your time to come? Plainly there's excessive uncertainty in human relationships when trying to make making predictions, but all you need to do here is make fair guesses. Your truthful anticipations, even if they might turn out to be inaccurate, still bear a lot of reality as they reveal your feelings. Your feelings will impact your actions, thereby inducing future changes in the direction of your relationships. Consequently, it's crucial to get aware of your truthful predictions as such awareness provides you the might to consciously alter what isn't working.

Chapter Six: Mixing of Reality

Give special attention to your feelings, as they bear their own anticipatory intelligence. Favorable emotions represent favorable predictions, and damaging emotions reveal damaging predictions. Occasionally you might feel like a relationship is waning even when everything appears great on the surface. Then you might have a word with your mate and find out that there are crucial overlooked issues you have to work through together. Once we bring those issues to the surface, even if we don't solve them immediately, the feeling of closeness returns again. I've learned to place a lot of trust in my feelings when it comes to relationships. When something seems wrong to me, I understand the best thing I may do is go to the other individual and explain that something doesn't appear right so that we may work together to sort it out. When you bring reality to your relationships, you establish closeness and trust. Untruth is clearly negative, but so is inattention. If you quit deliberately injecting fresh reality into your relationships on a steady basis, distance is produced by default. Reality isn't simply the absence of lying; reality is a crucial relationship activity. Take on whatever realities you discover about your relationships, even if you feel immobilized in your present situation. Don't buckle under to denial. If you feel blue and alone, take on those feelings. If you feel your union is headed for divorce, accept your truthful predictions.

If you feel totally stuck and powerless to change, accept that. Never shut your eyes to the reality. If you wish to develop beyond your present limitations, you have to first learn to quit resisting where you are. Lastly, it's crucial to accept the real nature of human relationships. All of them are assured to be temporary. Regardless how mighty your bonds are, they'll all sooner or later end in detachment or loss. No relationship may possibly live on, at least not in physical form. Let your awareness of this reality provide you a deeper appreciation of the individuals in your life. When you accept that your relationships are temporary, they'll become more treasured to you, and you'll be less likely to take others for granted. You'll see some facets of reality, affection, and might in all communication, but most individuals tend to lean to a great extent on one or two lines. What mixing of reality, affection, and might do you utilize to connect with other people? Recognize that your weakest line will be the source of many of your communication issues. You may really accomplish significant development in your relationships by learning to utilize your weakest line when communicating in addition to your fortes. In order to connect, we require a base level of compatibility. There has to be a little overlap in communication styles with which to build a link. If there's deficient overlap, a close connection merely won't settle in. In order to develop, however, we require a few differences in our techniques. Otherwise we swiftly hit a plateau in our power to connect.

Our similarities draw us together, but our differences help us develop. Now that you're mindful of the importance of reality, affection, and might, you are able to consciously direct the development of your relationships, and you are able to likewise diagnose issues. If you're in a relationship today, may you identify your main area of compatibility?

Do you connect on reality, sharing data and learning from one another? Do you connect on affection, expressing love and enjoying one another's company? Or do you connect on might, supporting and encouraging one another to accomplish your aspirations? If you buckle under to relationships that break you or make you feel ensnared, you're giving your might away. It's your responsibility to amend such situations, no matter the circumstances. Recognize that you may decide to leave at any time. There might be damaging consequences to doing so, like loss of money if you leave a scornful partner, but such issues are temporary. When you cast off disempowering relationships, you may expect to recover your might in time. Regrettably, the very nature of scornful connections is that they sabotage you to the point that it's difficult to even imagine being mighty again. If you discover yourself in a spot that weakens you and you don't decide to leave, then you're deciding to stay, which means you're deciding to ill-treat yourself.

A conscious relationship demands work and dedication on both sides. One person can't take on the whole thing solely. If you're spending more time battling resistance rather than sharing affection, you're better off letting go. Place yourself in a position to savor something more reciprocally rewarding, and don't settle for less than you're worth. Empowering yourself isn't a selfish action. Once you hold your relationships to the measure of empowerment, you grow more mighty, and your strength runs out to the individuals around you too. What do you do if your most disempowering relationships are with your own loved ones? There's no reward in remaining truehearted to somebody who dis-empowers you. When you sabotage yourself like that, you do the same to the individuals around you too, dragging everybody else down with you. Don't pressure yourself and other people to suffer from a misdirected sense of dedication. If you're a really truehearted individual, then give your allegiance to those who really merit it; don't blindly give it to those who claim it as their birthright. An uncommon or unlikely series of events leads us to the correct individuals at the correct times, and we get the spooky feeling we were in some way destined to meet. Before I experienced the mentality of unity, I could never walk into some random store and expect to be hugging somebody I'd never met previously. Be prepared for captivating social experiences as your alignment with unity increases.

I believe the reason this mentality is so effective is that when you assume a pre-existing connection, individuals tend to pick up on your receptiveness and react in a similar way. Seemingly, the best way to break the ice with somebody is to presume there never was any ice originally. This is particularly true of those who are really conscious and self-aware. Such individuals by nature react to friendly overtures from like-minded people, and injurious rejections are rare. If you approach somebody from a mentality of unity and are declined harshly, it's a safe bet the other individual isn't aligned with this idea and would consequently be incompatible with you anyhow. The nice thing about unity is that it by nature attracts other people who feel the same and separates out those who don't. The more you line up with unity, the more unity oriented relationships you'll draw in, thereby further reinforcing your experience. Social disciplining teaches you to center on the hazard of rejection when approaching somebody you've never met. Unity teaches you to center on the chances for connection. A rejection is a sign of incompatibility, so it can't truly be considered a sorry outcome. Then again, once a favorable connection is attained, there's the possibility that both individuals will be absolutely transformed for the better. This may hardly be considered a danger; rather, it's the sort of wager that's worth making repeatedly.

In addition to initiating fresh connections, be open to receiving advances from other people. When somebody makes an advance, react empathetically and kind. Be inviting and friendly. If you recognize the connection isn't correct for you, let the other individual down easily. When you determine it necessary to turn individuals down, be heedful not to dis-empower them. Be truthful but gentle. Then again, if you sense a well-matched connection off the bat, lower your shields, let your feelings lead you, and let the relationship grow as it may.   A lot of committed relationships buckle under to cheating or divorce as one or both mates end up feeling unplugged for too long. They let themselves connect with their main relationship partner but not with anybody else. Such ill-conceived loyalty becomes a controlling snare that knocks individuals out of alignment with unity. This produces strong cravings for truer connections, forcing individuals either to settle for reclusiveness or to look for fresh intimacy outside the main relationship. A feeling that such connections are incorrect makes the issue worse, causing individuals to lie about their affairs, therefore producing even more distance from unity.

When you're in a close relationship, value the fact that your mate isn't your property. Don't clutch others so tightly that you cut them off from being able to associate with anybody but you. In order to maximize your chances for conscious development, you must be open to molding new connections with an assortment of individuals, particularly when you're in a committed relationship.

Social disciplining tends to fail us in that area. We're encouraged to discover and wed a single partner, centering our deepest levels of physical and emotional intimacy on only one individual. However, simple observation tells us that relationships of this nature commonly fail, ending in breakup, divorce, or alienation. Even when the legal union doesn't stop and living together continues, the bond frequently stagnates and fails to gratify either individual's long-run emotional needs. Committed relationships call for placing a high value on your mates overall welfare. This includes respecting the need to connect with others, occasionally casually and other times more closely. If your main relationship prevents you from connecting deeply with other people, you've a cage, not a witting partnership. Human relationships are an enormous source of learning and growth. Our biggest rewards in life develop there, as do our most intriguing problems. Relationships may be complicated and perplexing at times, but as you'll soon learn reality, affection, and might bring an elegant simplicity to the picture, helping us build witting, loving associations. We have an assortment of intimate relationship openings to pick from. A few individuals prefer to be totally monogamous, opting for one romantic partner till ultimately separated by dying. Other people choose serial monogamy, going through an assortment of mates in succession.

Still other people like polyamorous relationships, preferring multiple partners at the same time. And lastly, a few choose celibacy and channel their romantic energies elsewhere.

You have freedom to guide the course of your relationships however you like, with the caution that your partners willingly decide to share those things with you. As a few of the ideas in this book conflict with mainstream social disciplining, you might come across parts you take issue with, and that's all right. Apart from demonstrating how to apply the rules we've talked about in this course to your relationships, I don't aspire to convince you to alter your particular values to meet my own. I do, all the same, wish to challenge you to question your suppositions about relationships and make your own witting selections, even though your preferences might differ from mine. Our lives are filled with a myriad of common relationship forms: loved ones, acquaintances, friends, colleagues, intimate partners, opponents, and strangers. No matter your present situation, reality, affection, this might may help you better all of these. But lets' take another look in this, how can a man actually attach the woman of his dreams? Women, just like men, have varying opinions about what makes someone attractive physically and mentally. Also just like men, for some women looks are more important than others.

And every woman thinks different men are attractive. For many women, appearance is not a major factor in dating a man. Many women find it is most important to be romantically involved with a good man who is good to her. Someone that can make her laugh, hold an interesting conversation, and make life more fun and interesting. With this in mind, you'll need to take a close look at yourself, complete the worksheets, and focus on your top attributes when trying to attract a woman. When you are around single women, you shouldn't worry that you will be shot down if you approach them. Most women are reasonable and normal, and a simple friendly conversation will not end negatively. Women like positive, noncreepy attention from men, and many dress up to boost their self confidence in the dating arena. Women will tell you if they are not interested. You shouldn't feel nervous about approaching an attractive woman and striking up a conversation. If she's taken or not interested, she'll simply say so. No harm done. It's best to develop the attitude that taking small risks will have a big payoff. If you don't try you will never know. When looking at yourself, and listening to your internal thoughts, consider lightening up a little bit. Men are often very hard on themselves. It's important to understand that thinking this way is self-defeating, and a sure way to line yourself up for failure, simply because you talk yourself out of being successful. If you think self-confidence, you will act self-confident, which is attractive to women.

Confidence will make you feel more comfortable about approaching a woman, and will benefit your dating life significantly. When most couples make the decision to be part of a committed relationship, there are a lot of mental, physical and legal issues that would have to be dealt with in order for them to take the next step in life as one unit rather than two individual existences. These issues can sometimes be very complicated and in some cases requiring long term commitments of which it would be very difficult to evade or get out of. Making a life time commitment to someone is not an easy thing to do and requires a lot of thought and adjustments on both parts. The changes made are significant and if the relationship eventually runs its course or the notion of calling it quits is very evident, then losses will be incurred on both sides which can sometimes be rather hard to recover from. Both emotionally and financially, both individual will have to start all over again and this is certainly not a very pleasant experience to have to eventually face. Therefore making the right choice from the very beginning will help both parties avoid such negative possibilities eventually. As we already mentioned before, We can say that sex is not a sin. It is one of the precious gifts from God. That's why we have to give priority to our life partner in order to have sexual satisfaction. This is a well known fact, sex is looked at in the most negative way, but it's truly a gift.

Chapter Seven: Spiritual Connection

By developing a spiritual connection, you gain security through the strong belief that you're not all alone in the universe, even at those times when you feel temporarily disjointed from others. You feel more and more safe as you come to trust that there's a source you are able to always turn to in times of trouble. Serenity is the result of sensing a deep, enduring sense of security and safety. The more trust and reliance you develop in spirituality, the simpler it becomes to cope without fear or concern with the inevitable challenges life bestows. It isn't that you abandon your self or your will to such a power; instead you merely learn that you are able to "let go" and trust when you feel stuck with an issue and don't understand how to go forward. Learning how to relinquish when answers to issues aren't directly apparent may go a long way towards reducing worry and anxiety in your life. Serenity is what arises in the absence of such anxiety. As you develop a spiritual relationship, you come to recognize that there's something great in you. You're part of the universe. You're great, lovable, and worthy of regard just by virtue of the fact that you're here. This fruition may improve the way you view yourself and will help you to better your ego and what you believe of yourself. You're still inherently good and worthwhile. Your own judgings of yourself, however damaging, don't ultimately count if you're a creation of the universe as much as everything else.

The most cardinal characteristic of spirituality is that it provides you an experience of unconditional love. This is a sort of love which differs from romantic love or even average friendship. It means an absolute caring for the well-being of another with no conditions. That's, regardless how another individual seems or acts, you've compassion and treasure them without judging. As you acquire a deeper connection, you come to feel higher degrees of unconditional love in your life. You sense your heart opening more easily to individuals and their interests. You feel freer of judging them or of making comparisons amidst them. Unconditional love comes out both in your expanded capacity to give love to other people and to have more of it coming into your life. You start to experience less dread and more joy in your life and help to inspire other people to experience their own capacity for unconditional love. This sort of love in addition to manifests itself through the experience of having everything you require in your life to get on with what you wish to do. Acquiring a relationship with spirituality will supply you with guidance for arriving at decisions and figuring out issues. Spirituality has a universal wisdom that goes beyond what you are able to accomplish through your own reason. In traditional faiths this has been referred to as the "divine intelligence." Through connecting, you are able to draw upon this higher wisdom to help you settle all kinds of troubles. By learning to invite guidance, you'll be surprised to discover that every sincere request eventually is answered. And the caliber of that answer commonly exceeds what you may have worked out through your own conscious intellect or will.

If you trust in endurance of the spirit and that you are able to recover, you might have fewer anxieties and even reach a place of much richer and greater admiration for all of the chances, blessings and lessons you've had and will have in this life. You'll pull through the closure process with Appreciation for the great experiences you recall and the lessons acquired; with gratefulness for the enrichments accumulated in your life so far; and with acute anticipation for the graces yet to come. In this life there is transience in all experiences. Recognizing an end will bear on every and each relationship we have, including the elemental end of our relationship with all we have lived in this life, helps us to treasure every experience a great deal more. This awareness might be one of the biggest benefits of transitioning through the healing process. This is a branching out of our positive cognizance. That is, when we understand we're safe and need not fear our past experiences - which is for a lot of people very difficult- then all additional stress and fears in our lives become nothing more than added lessons. We understand that everything in our lifetime is manageable; there's nothing we have to worry about or fear. We may than accept everything in our life as a lesson. Rather than saying, "Oh, my goodness! How will I handle this challenge?" we can state, "Hmmm! I"m curious what intriguing lessons I'll get from this invitation to look deeper inside myself?" or "I question what I'll discover to clear up next from the file drawer that this hurdle is directing me towards?" How do you seduce a woman with spirituality?

Understanding what a woman is looking for in a man is the first secret to seducing a woman. For many men, the concept of how to seduce a woman is simply a mystery. It's understandable, though. Men and women differ in so many ways that it's difficult for many of us, male or female, to really grasp how to get inside the mind of someone who is a near polar opposite of us. You have to know what makes the other person tick, what really gets them going, catches their attention, and keeps it. And that is, ultimately, the key to success when it comes to seduction. For women, that tends to be an easier task. Now, don't get me wrong, there are plenty of women who don't know how to seduce a man. But on the average it seems to be a little easier for women to figure out what you men want. On the other hand, men may not be so quick to figure the opposite sex out. It's not surprising though, women are complicated creatures. However, what women want is not all that all that difficult to accommodate once you know what it is. And when you do know, put that knowledge to use and it will surely pay off! If I have you scratching your head in wonder now, don't worry. It's all about to come together. There are a few things you must understand about a woman to know how to seduce her. It's not just roses and chocolates or a nice meal and a bottle of wine. Though, don't get me wrong, those are all great. The true key to seducing a woman isn't a mere laundry list to check off, step by step. It's more a guidebook on the path you must follow to completely seduce a woman, mind, body and soul.

Now if the thought of attempting to seduce a woman's mind or soul has you ready to run for cover, take heart, it's not as difficult as you may think. What really gets a woman going is much simpler than you may have ever imagined. Understanding the differences between the sexes will help give you a better foundation on which to build your knowledge of women. And believe me, there's no better way to get to a woman than by truly understanding her. Once you can get inside her mind, it's all downhill from there. Communication is ultimately the most important aspect of seducing a woman. Like so many other aspects of our lives, effective communication is the key to success. You want to take the time to really get to know her and what she's looking for. This will benefit you greatly when it comes to pleasing her, so don't think that getting to know your woman is a pointless, grueling task of learning a bunch of useless information. Patience when seducing your woman is very important. Being in a hurry will only prove to damage any good you could've done by learning anything at all about your woman. When it comes to seducing a woman, take it slow. Women want a man to take his time, not just rush in for the brass ring. A woman wants to know that you aren't just playing her for sex. And the best way to prove yourself is to take your time. Women want to feel special. Being romantic makes women feel special. I know, I know, you're probably grumbling now, right? Well, let me tell you, romance is a must. If you want to seduce your woman you have to be romantic.

It proves that you care, that you want to please her and that you know how to treat a woman right. Romance will take you a long way in seducing a woman. Knowing what you want in a woman is imperative. You need to know what you want before you can ever expect to be happy. Taking the time to figure out what you want will save you a lot of time and heartache later on. Superficial tendencies tie in with knowing what you want in a woman. Being superficial is a major pitfall for many people. Whether it be admiring a vehicle for its looks and not how economical it is or how long it will last, or judging another person based on the clothes they're wearing or the neighborhood they live in. Knowing what you really want in a woman and being able to overcome and superficial tendencies you may have will really benefit you. Amazingly, knowing what you want will pay off in another respect, as well. It will make you happier and more confident. Both of these qualities happen to be very attractive to women. Women like a man with a good attitude, which generally comes from being happy and confident. Not just a nice guy, but a guy with a positive and upbeat attitude. Self-confident men attract more women. Why, you ask? Self-confidence is sexy. Yes, that's right. A man who's confident in himself is more likely to be successful. And success equals satisfaction. When a man is satisfied he makes a better partner. Being sensitive is another important element to seducing a woman.

Women like a man who's capable of being tough and tender. I know this sounds like a tall order, but I think it's something that every man has in him, he might just be afraid to show it. Or maybe he's just not aware that he has a sensitive side. Setting the mood for romance is a great way to seduce women. You don't have to wait for it to happen, you can make it happen. The effort alone will score points with your lady, not to mention making you feel good about what you've done! It may sound like a tall order, but once you know women it's not difficult to pull something like this off without much effort at all. Finding out as much as you can about the woman in your life is essential. Simply learning what you can about women in general isn't enough. After all, just like you men, all women are different. There are some things that most women or most men look for or want, but each of us are unique. Learning what your woman wants as an individual will allow you to seduce her the way she wants. As you can clearly see now, seducing a woman is much more about her mind than her body. Don't get me wrong, her body is important, too. But when it comes right down to it, the seduction of a woman starts in her mind, moves to her soul and ends with her body. Understanding what your woman wants, likes and needs will enable you to seduce her completely. When it comes to seducing a woman confidence is vital. Women equate selfconfidence with the ability to be successful.

While many men believe that women look for successful men because they're likely to make more money, that's simply not true. Women look for successful men because they're more likely to be satisfied. That's right, satisfied. You may be wondering what a man being satisfied has to do with anything. Let me explain. Women know that men who are satisfied with themselves are less likely to go out looking for someone to satisfy them and are more stable. And in a relationship that means a man will be less likely to cheat, or change jobs frequently or get himself into any number of other compromising situations. Remember, most women are looking for a man who will be their partner as well as their lover. Not only do they want a partner when it comes to things like companionship, decision-making and finances, but in the bedroom, as well. In order to effectively seduce a woman you must make her feel as though you're equals. This is important because she needs to know that the seduction is 50 – 50, that both of you are experiencing the same level of pleasure. When it comes to confidence it seems there are two kinds of people, those who have it, and those who don't. Although on the surface this may be true, everyone has the potential to be self confident. If you're a naturally confident person you may find it easy to approach people you don't know, easy to stand up in front of a room full of strangers and give a speech and easy to open up to a woman you're attracted to. However, if you're not naturally confident this may all seem difficult.

While you may be ready to throw your hands up in defeat, don't be so quick to give up. Just because you're not the kind of guy to jump up on stage and give a speech doesn't mean you're not confident enough to impress a woman. Take heart in knowing that you're a good person, smart, funny, good at your job, loving, considerate or whatever else you find to be positive character traits that you have. Not all women are looking for a CEO or brain surgeon. Women just want a man who's confident with who he is, what he knows and what he has to offer to a relationship with women. If you're unsure of your strengths, try making a list of the qualities you have that you feel good about and the areas you feel may need some improvement. You don't need to delve head-long into psychology, just take some time to reflect on yourself. You can use your strengths to build on areas that need a little work. Just be sure not to dwell on any areas you feel you may be lacking in, as this will only serve to make you feel even less confident. Not only is self-confidence important when you first meet someone, it's important when you're getting to know one another. You need to feel self confident enough to be open with women about yourself. Women don't like it when a man is afraid to tell them his thoughts and feelings. That sort of behavior is sure to get a woman's defenses up and won't get you very far in seducing her. Remember, seduction should be built on the premise that both of you will be equals, so sharing your minds is as important as sharing your bodies.

Confident men generally make better lovers, too. A man who feels stable in his work, relationships and friendships tends to feel more sure of himself in the bedroom. This works wonders in seducing a woman. A man who comes across as confident is much more likely to make a woman feel comfortable with him and is more likely to respond positively to his advances. Not to mention the fact that knowing that you have what it takes to please a woman makes you a more self assured lover who will be less reserved and more passionate. Being self confident not only makes a woman more likely to find you attractive, but it also makes you feel good about yourself. When you feel good about yourself you're more likely to have another fine character trait: self respect. Why is this important? If you have self-respect you're more likely to be respectful of others. This inevitably will perpetuate a life-long cycle of self-confidence, self respect and respect for others that will serve you and your love life well. A person who is incapable of loving and respecting themselves is incapable of loving or respecting others. A lack of self respect will send up a red flag to most women and will kill your chances of ever having a relationship with that one, special woman. We all want respect, and by all I mean all people. As I said before, if you can't respect yourself you can't respect women, and if you can't respect them, you can't love them. And love, after all, is what we're all looking for. We want it, need it and deserve it…everybody does.

Although we don't have to be in love to have sex, the idea behind seduction goes beyond just having sex. It's taking the time to please someone completely, not just get them in bed. So, even though you may not love the person you're seducing, you have to, at the very least, care enough about them to want to please them. And for women, in order to seduce them you have to respect yourself and them. In order to seduce a woman you have to be capable of respecting her completely, mind, body and soul. Women want to know that there's no chance you're going to try to get inside their head and play mind games with them. Women want to know that when you put your hands on their body that you're doing it to make both of them feel good, not just yourself. And they want to know that when you seduce them it's because you want to feel a connection to them that goes beyond just the physical connection you get from sex. When it comes to self-confidence and self-respect, there is nothing that will substitute for them. You must exude these qualities in order for a woman to be able to pick up on them. We don't like to search for those character traits. If we have to chip away at layer after layer before we find what we're looking for, we're much more likely to lose interest. So put your best foot forward when it comes to impressing a woman. Although women are not overly impatient creatures, women don't want to have to wait too long to see what kind of person you are. If you're too reserved a woman will generally start to worry that you may have something that you're trying to hide, which might just cause her to move on rather than running the risk of being hurt.

So flash that smile, work that charm and give your lady a chance to see how wonderful you really are. You will most definitely be rewarded in the long run. Knowing what you're looking for in a woman can be quite difficult. Many men think use a certain color hair of a certain physical feature as a standard by which they choose women to approach. This will not serve you well if you plan on seducing a woman. When it comes to seducing a woman, I can't stress enough that you must have something in common with the woman you're trying to seduce. If you don't having something in common with them other than a mutual physical attraction, chances are very, very good that the seduction will not work. For this reason, if no other, it's important that you take the time to figure out what you really want in woman aside of looks. In order to find out what you're really looking for in a woman, you need to take the time to consider the complete person, not just the body. You need to take into consideration things like personality, interests, ambitions and then looks. You're probably wondering why I listed those traits in the order I did. Let me explain. If you consider looks first it will tend to cloud your judgment on all the other traits. Men tend to be very easily visually stimulated. For this reason, what excites them at first sight tends to be what they think they want. However, if you consider what you want in the other areas, the looks may not be so important.

Chapter Eight: Seduction

You may find that a woman with a great personality that likes football and racing as much as you do and who takes her career as a human resources director seriously, but who happens to be a brunette with only an average build, would suit you just fine. Personality, intelligence, ambition, sense of humor and interests play a much bigger role in attraction than just physical appearance. The best way to figure out what you really want is to do a lot of soul-searching and be very objective. You might want to get a piece of paper and a pen and make a list. Sit back and think of all the women that you know. Make a list of all the traits and characteristics of these women that you find attractive, discounting looks. Then make another list of all the traits that any of them have that you don't like or make them unattractive to you, again discounting looks. When you've finished, take time to really examine your lists. You may be truly surprised to see the results. This is a fine example of thinking like a woman, which is a great step in the right direction when seducing a woman, by the way. Women tend to give greater consideration to personality, intelligence, and the other traits I mentioned earlier, than they do to physical appearance. This is not to say that physical attraction doesn't hold any weight, but it's much less important when you find someone that's a great match for you in all the other areas.

I'm sure you must be wondering what I'm getting at with all of this. Let me explain. When it comes to seducing a woman, as I mentioned earlier, it starts in her mind. In order to get inside a woman's mind you must be a good match for her where certain traits are concerned. You must have personalities that compliment one another. Once you've found someone who has an agreeable personality then you can strike up a conversation and move on to see if you have common interests. When you find that you have common interests, then you have something to work with. Now you can move on to having good conversation that will make her feel more comfortable with you, which is a huge step in the right direction. Believe me, taking the time to figure out what you really want in a woman will pay off in more ways than one. It's not just a matter of being able to have a conversation with them, it's much more. The mere knowledge that you know what you're looking for in a woman will make you a much more confident person. And, as I discussed with you earlier, confidence is essential, not to mention sexy. Knowing what you want, in itself, is attractive to women. The minute women sense that a man knows what he's looking for it scores big points with them. As I mentioned earlier, women not overly impatient, but women don't like to spend time trying to get to know you only to find out women are not your type. When we know what women are looking for and so do you, that moves things along in the right direction much more quickly and easily.

You will probably be very shocked to discover that simply being with the right kind of person can be quite exciting. Something about personalities that mesh sets things in motion in a way that you could've only imagined before. You'll feel much more at ease. And when you feel at ease with us you'll be more prone to opening up to us and sharing your thoughts and feelings, which women find very, very attractive. This knowledge also plays into another aspect of seduction and that is making your woman feel special. Being compatible allows you to communicate better which, ultimately, allows you to get to know one another better. The more you know about women the more you can romance them. You'll know what women like, what makes them feel special, and what really makes them feel wanted. Not only will women enjoy this, but you will, too. You'd be amazed to discover that all the mushy, romantic things that you may have avoided over the years will give you a great deal of pleasure, too. And the rewards you will receive from them after planning that especially romantic evening or weekend will be sure to please you. As I'm sure you've noticed by now, all of these tips that I'm giving you are interconnected in one way or another. And this tip is no exception. Knowing what you want affects many different aspects of how you seduce a woman. Knowing what you want makes you more confident. Being more confident makes us feel more comfortable with you, thereby opening the lines of communication, which leads to a greater knowledge of one another.

You'll see later on that all of these tips work together in one respect or another. But bear in mind, none of them will work all on their own. I know this tip may sound very cliché, but it's true. At some point or another women are all guilty of judging something, or someone, based on appearance alone. While it's not right, women still seem to have that tendency to be superficial. This type of behavior can be very detrimental when it comes to seducing a woman. Women like to be appreciated for who they are, not what they look like. Even those women who have great physical beauty don't necessarily want to be judged on that characteristic alone. Let me explain a few reasons why to help you understand women better. Women keep the thought in the back of their mind that one day they may want to have a child. If and when they become pregnant, look at all the changes their body goes through. The mere fact that their body has to expand at a very rapid pace to accommodate the growth of the baby is frightening. And the knowledge that their figure may never be the same is equally frightening. Women don't want to worry that if they become pregnant their man is going to find our swollen belly and puffy ankles repulsive. Women want to know that despite our girth you'll find women beautiful. If a woman gets the slightest hint that you're basing your interest in her more on her physique than anything else you probably won't get very far with her.

Another thought that women have is that eventually we all get older and less youthful in appearance. Wrinkles, gray hair and gravity are of great concern to women. We know that in general, a man is considered more distinguished looking when his hair takes on the salt and pepper look, whereas women merely look old. A few wrinkles on a man are no big deal, but for women the first sign of a wrinkle is cause to consider botox treatment, or more. Society has made women terribly self conscious. And while not all of women are willing to go to extremes to maintain a youthful appearance, women surely don't want to be criticized for aging naturally. This is important to bear in mind when considering what you truly believe is important in a woman. If looks is top on your list it will surely lead to a very dissatisfying experience for you, and your woman. I'm not trying to say that you have to resolve to be happy with someone you find utterly unattractive. We all have preferences in looks, personality and many other traits that we have to abide by. It's a matter of compatibility. But what we do have to take into consideration is that attraction is not just a matter of physical appearance. As I mentioned earlier, there's more to a person than just their body. And most of what attracts to people to each other is about what's inside, not outside. So take the time to find out what's inside before you discount women based on what's outside.

I'm sure you're wondering why I'm spending so much time on this. Well, it's simple really. When attempting to seduce a woman you have to make her feel comfortable with you. But beyond comfort is something even more important. A woman must know that she can trust you with her heart. To make a woman feel that way you must be willing to accept everything about her, including the fact that inevitably time will take its toll on her body. If women know that their man loves who we are more than how they look it makes it very easy for them to trust him. To be successful with this it's imperative that you find traits in a woman that are more important to you than physical beauty. Concentrate on things like charm, intelligence, honesty, loyalty, ambition, humor or anything else that you find attractive in a personality. Next, give thought to how this factors in to the overall relationship. Take time to think about what will make you want to maintain a long-term relationship a woman. Now think 10 years into the future. Consider what you and she will look like then. Do you think you'll she'll still be as physically fit and physically attractive as she is now? What about your physical appearance? Chances are neither of you will be as physically fit and physically attractive as you are right now. But take some time now to consider all of the other characteristics that you find attractive. Chances are they haven't changed.

And if they have, generally it's for the better. Spending time with a person whose personality compliments your own makes a very positive influence on both people. It enhances every aspect of who they are. So you can see that despite the fact that neither of you will remain as attractive physically, when it comes to mental and emotional attraction there is much to look forward to in the future. And if you can tell a woman that you're attracted to her and mean that you're attracted to all of her, then you're on the right path to seducing her. The best way to make a woman understand that you're not superficial is to compliment her without constantly referring to her body. Women would prefer you compliment them on their body less and the rest of them more. This makes them more confident that you appreciate everything about them, not just their appearance. If you tell a woman she's sexy, she'll instantly assume you're referring to her body, never mind the fact that she has a very sexy personality. You can be successful at this by complimenting women on how good they are at their job, how funny they are, what a great smile they have or any number of other things. This doesn't mean you should never compliment them on their physical appearance. Just find a nice balance. There's one last thing to remember about avoiding the tendency to be superficial. When you open yourself up to the idea that you could find more about a woman attractive than just her body, it opens you up to being able to experience a new level of connection with a woman.

As I mentioned in the previous tip, you'll be amazed to find that being with the right kind of person, rather than the person who looks the best, will allow you to experience the pleasure of being with someone whose personality really meshes with yours. This will inevitably make you and her both more comfortable, allowing you to share openly and honestly with one another. By doing this you will be able to get inside her mind and really learn about her. Now that you can see how much there is about a woman that you can find attractive and alluring let's take the time to discuss what this characteristic will mean to your woman. Not only will she feel more comfortable with you and feel like she can trust you, but she will feel that you're not overly critical or judgmental. That's very important to them. She'll also feel that even if her looks fade with time that there's still much more about her that you love and appreciate. She will also feel that the two of you have that in common, since women tend to look for characteristics in a man like personality, loyalty, honesty and ambition first, then looks later. When a woman feels that you'll accept her and love her just the way she is, she can envision you being happy with the way she is in the future, too. And with her feeling this way about you, you will be well on your way to being able to seduce your woman, mind, body and soul. The kind of attitude we have affects literally every aspect of our lives. Whether it's our work, social life, love life or health, our attitude plays a part in it all.

When it comes to seducing a woman, attitude plays a very big role in how successful, or unsuccessful you are. If you have a positive attitude you're more likely to attract women more easily than a guy with a negative attitude. Being positive and upbeat shows in nearly everything you do, as does being negative and glum. Women are much more likely to choose the positive, upbeat guys. Let me take a little time to explain how attitude affects your success in attracting and seducing a woman. First, a positive attitude reflects confidence and self respect. As we already discussed, confidence and self respect are vital. A positive attitude also directly affects how other people feel when they're around you. For example, have you ever had a friend or co-worker who was always down or pessimistic? If you have, did you notice that after a while his or her mood started making you feel down or uncomfortable or irritable? Chances are it's happened to all of them. So remember, if for no other reason than to not be a dark cloud hanging over everyone's head, try your best to be positive and have a good attitude. But it goes much further than that. When you're trying to make your best impression on a woman, being negative will not work. You have to feel good before you can make anyone else feel good. You have to radiate the same kinds of feelings you want to receive. If you're not giving off those positive vibes women'll pick up on it and most likely steer clear of you.

As I mentioned earlier, your attitude affects all aspects of your life. If you have a negative attitude you're less likely to be successful in many things, including work. Women like to find a man who's stable. Part of what we judge stability on is your work. No, this doesn't mean you need to be a rocket scientist. It simply means that if you're changing jobs every couple of months, or getting let go for poor attitude or poor performance, which is directly affected by your attitude, then women are going to think twice before women get involved with you. Remember, women are looking for a partner; a 50 – 50 relationship. There's another way that your attitude can affect your success with women. All people like to have emotional support in a relationship, but no one likes to be the sole provider of that emotional support. When women sense that a man has a negative attitude it makes them wonder if he's going to be emotionally needy. A sure way to nix any hope of seducing a woman is to be emotionally needy. It sets up a child-like image of you in her mind and will make it very difficult for her to see you as a seductive man. Now this is not to say that women'll never be supportive of your emotional needs. Women like all aspects of their relationship with a man to be as equal as possible. And women are very willing to lend emotional support, just as women would expect it from you, too. There just needs to balance in your attitude. Everyone is entitled to have a bad day now and again. And having a bad day is not going to doom your chances at seducing them.

Chapter Nine: Flourish Andy Thrive

Male and female courtship signals have been studied, and the basic conclusions are that these signals are completely unconscious. The more you consciously understand the signals, the better and more successful you will be when courting the object of your desire, whether it is the man or woman of your dreams. To master the art of successful flirting, you have to feel good about yourself first. Be confident. Be yourself, or else you will look deceitful or desperate. Flirting can be utilized in just about anything, not just in attracting the opposite sex, but also in attaining just about anything you want in your life. This can be described as good flirting. Good flirting should be done with a precise understanding of what you really want, coupled with positive sensations. A simple touch to the body can have a thousand different meanings depending on how you perceive the power of touch in body language. It is a basic need to be touched. We definitely need to be stroked and have physical contact with other people to survive. As we mature, we continue to heed that need of touching and being touched. Touch can convey respect and trust, and is also a way to differentiate power between people. Touching as an ingredient of body language can be a powerful tool if done with finesse, with precision, and with accuracy. You must learn the art of touching in order to send your signals to the other person.

Timing is important, as some people will react negatively if you touch them too soon or too much. It has to be done at the right time in a suitable way, or the result would not be one that you expect. Be keen to the circumstances and the mood. You can determine the appropriateness of your touch and your ability to adjust to the circumstances, by how your receiver reacts to it. If the person seems to lean or get closer to you, you've made the right move. But if the person seems to back off, this means you did not touch properly, so you have to make some adjustments. Love figures in a big way in everyone's lives. Some dream about it, some romanticize it and others deny it. But it is an always in vogue topic of discussion. Though the one 'right' person theory might be a myth but that does not mean that there is not more than one right person for you. So how does one define that all encompassing 'right' factor in a partner? Well it might be defined as a kind of compatibility, which allows you to flourish and thrive in each other's company. It is probably the quality, which makes it a solid team, where it is not the individual but the final end,which matters. Such bonds are established on far stronger stuff than mere attraction, though this is a large and significant part of it. It is rather based on simple facts of common ideals, dreams and beliefs. There has always been a tendency to exalt the entire notion of love in all mediums, literature, television or theatre.

But this entirely focuses that early phase of devotion passion and jubilation. But this stage in real life is short in duration as soon the high is gone and matters more practical have to be handled. So, if one mistakes this initial stage of exhilarating romantic moments for the actual deal then it can lead to the downfall of the relationship. But this romantic phase serves a good purpose in reminding and holding exemplary importance regarding the potential that this relationship can possess when bad times are nigh. Today happiness has become such a sort after commodity that people will do and believe anything for that. They will agree to any terms so that they never have to feel pain, be hurt or get disappointed. That is why they are ready to jump at and grab any clauses that prevent these in their relationships, and make them work anyhow. Friends, family, neighbors and the amazing sights and sounds of the great wide world full of possibilities await one if only one makes the effort to appreciate. But one only notices all the variety and beauty when one is in love. Only a soul mate who can share your experience makes everything worthwhile. If you are or have been in a long term relationship, you would be well conversant with the pains and pleasures involved. There are moments of happiness interspersed with bouts of doubt and difference of opinions between you and your partner.

It has been seen that the in first few months or may be even in the first few years the couple are blissfully happy. They are head over heels in love with each other and cannot find any flaw in their mate however hard they try. When in a relationship, we badly try to rediscover ourselves. The questions like, "why we exist?", "for whom do we exist?", "does that person actually deserve me or do I deserve him/her?" keep gnawing at our existence. Also, the very thought of getting united with that person seems to cast us into perpetual tension and we spend sleepless nights trying to find an answer. The challenge before us is whether we would be able to put up with that person all are life or vice versa. If you plan to be in a long term relationship, you need to do a good groundwork. It takes years to make a relationship work. At the very beginning, you should be clear about what you want from your partner and what you think you can do for him/her. Take time and develop the optimum amount of trust that is required to make your relationship work. Compassion is another essential element which you need to feel for your partner, but that would take time. Thus, it's important to spend quality time with that person. The very thought of being with this same person all your life might frighten you but give yourself time to review things and then, decide accordingly. You should always divide your time so that your career or personal life does not get in each other's ways.

As much as it is important to stay focused on your work, you should always reserve time for the physical aspect of your relationship. It is a very important aspect and even if you find yourself not being able to devote time to it, there must always be a possibility of it happening. More importantly, you should be looking forward to that. As time elapses, both of you get know each other intimately. You learn to respect and approve of each other as living beings. You discover your partner's likes and dislikes on intimate emotional level what gives them joy, what problems they are trying to sort out and you reinstate the good, and strive to assist them in their attempts to surmount whatever difficult things they are dealing with. Spirituality, on the other hand, bears on to the common experience behind these assorted viewpoints. It's an experience calling for an awareness of and relationship with something that exceeds your personal self as well as the mortal order of things. Spiritual development may often be a hard and rocky road. At those times, words of spiritual encouragement may be the perfect thing to help you feel better. Saying a day-to-day affirmation is an excellent way to stay in a state of spiritual wellness. You and I are so bombed with negativity day-after-day. Positive and healing affirmations may help you feel better about your life and more optimistic about your future. Being with other spiritual individuals is among the best things you are able to do to maintain an attitude of spiritual wellness. A lot of individuals are so centered on the material aspects of life. They believe spirituality is something you only do one day a week.

An acceptable spiritual life will start with a complete shift in relation between God and the person; not a judicial change simply, but a conscious and knowledgeable change affecting the person's entire nature. Dismiss the negative notions you have of spiritual individuals. Faith has acquired a bad reputation due to flawed individuals, not a flawed God. No one is perfect. Try to remember that God loves these individuals even as much as God loves you. Worry about yourself and your spiritual maturation and leave the rest to God. First of all, you should be sure that your soul mate is the only person in the world with whom you can live your life. If you are confused about your choice then, things will start to get troubled. Even if you have some differences but exaggerating them and making them an issue is not the right way. You should always pay attention to your partner and make them believe that he or she is special for you. Spirituality is something which is a necessary ingredient to make relationships stronger. Spirituality is missing from this world and this is the biggest reason that peace calmness and harmony is also missing from our lives. It is not necessary to believe in certain religion to practice spirituality instead you can practice it through lots of methods for example if you just stop hunting your negative and materialistic desires then, you will get spirituality of one kind and once you achieve that then, you will know that there are so many things which are inter related to those desires and without those desires you can make so many things straight and more realistic in your life.

You'll know when you make contact with spiritual Power. Different individuals sense the presence of Power in assorted ways. Many will feel heat, or pressure, or will perceive a keener luminance. A few will feel a sense of cold, or a light airiness surrounding them. When you make contact, then you're ready for the next step, which is to affirm what you're asking for as if it were already true. You'll commonly want to create your affirmative prayer before you begin, however. Whatsoever you want out of life, you are able to have. Do whatever you can on the physical level to get it, and add the help of the spiritual level with affirmative prayers. Negative thoughts make you feel awful anxious, sad, blue, hopeless, guilty, mad. Rather than being overwhelmed by these feelings, you are able to learn to use them as a prompt for action. Notice when your mood shifts for the worse, and look back at what was working through your mind at that minute. Over the course of a few days, you'll become more sensitive to shifts in your feelings, and to the thoughts that set them off. You might well find that the same thoughts happen over and over. Depression comes with negative thoughts. To block off negative thoughts ignoring simply doesn't last or truly work. One must work at defeating negative thoughts and this is done when you switch negative thoughts into favorable thoughts. Make it a habit in your daily life to center on what you want in life not on what you don't want in life. When those damaging thoughts come into your mind substitute them with a positive thought of what you're wanting for yourself.

There is nothing wrong with wanting so much more out of life. Sex and pleasure are two things that are not negative, but are looked at that way. The whole world can be divided into two types of people. We are speaking of the achievers here – but with achievement we don"t refer to those who have become multimillionaires or beyond! We are speaking about ordinary people who achieve the usual things in life. Such people can be divided into two groups – those who carry on in a purpose-driven manner and those who carry on in an action-driven manner. At the end of it all, it doesn"t really matter which side of the fence you are sitting on. Both these are paths to success. When you are living in a purpose-driven manner, you are streamlining your line so as to achieve specific purposes in life. You set your goals and these goals become the be-all-and-end-all of your life. All your efforts are dedicated toward achieving these goals. You might want to do that in the short term or in the long term, but most of the efforts in your life are targeted at attaining those objectives. People who live an action oriented life do things in a different manner. They do set goals as well, but for them it is not the product but the process that"s more important. They plan their processes for the sake of carrying out their processes. They are quite dedicated in what they do. Though it will make them quite happy to achieve what they are looking for, it is the journey that interests them more than the destination.

For example, if your purpose in life is to become a millionaire, and everything that you do and plan is toward achieving that goal, you are living a purpose-driven life. For you, it doesn"t matter what you do to reach there. Your activities in life are just a means to the end. But, if you are action-driven, what you do to become a millionaire will really matter to you. You will be completely engrossed in the things you pursue to reach the goal. You might learn something to reach there. You might start a business. You might network with people. make a mental note that God wants to bless us all in abundance and theres' no reason for any of us to want the most out of life, as long as we believe it, we can achieve it! Purposes are the next step of aspirations. But they aren"t the next automatic step. They are a step that comes only after to begin working in that direction. You have to start working in order to convert your purposes into aspirations. Actually, this is the beginning of your action-driven life, but you should know that you still have to go a long way ahead. The best way you can make your aspirations into purposes is by setting milestones for yourself. You cannot achieve what you dream at a short notice. Most people make the biggest mistake of their lives here. They dream, but then they decide that their dreams are too fantastic and never take any steps in the direction of their fulfillment. That isn"t how an action-driven life works at all. Why, that's not even a purpose-driven life! Have the life that god wants you to have, life should not be a stuggle when you believe.

A sense of freedom is something that we all want to achieve. Being independent in whatever aspect it may be definitely boosts our confidence and makes us do better in life. We must all be equipped with this certain type of positive energy within us in order to have a major shift in the way we live. Spirituality may be associated with religious things and ceremonies but in this case, it does not necessarily mean that we should be hooked to a religion. Experiencing this state would mean that one's consciousness is awakened. This enables the person to see the person one really is and become aware of the capabilities and limitations attached to it. This makes the person become happy and contented with the person that he is. Thus, he is able to take care of and understand himself more than he used to. Being spiritually empowered makes a person aware of what makes him happy and makes him more sensitive to what would make other people happy. It is not only enough to seek help from other people by using meditative and alternative therapies on your way to spiritual empowerment. It would help much if you were able to become the personal coach to your own self so that you can criticize easily if you make any mistakes. Having an enriched and empowered spiritual life would mean that a person is able to accept one's self, no matter the limitations he has. When you fail to accept that and tend to blame yourself for things because you are a weak person who has too little capabilities, then you should start to tutor yourself into forgetting that part.

Chapter Ten: Spiritual Development

Keep in mind that you are in the road to spiritual empowerment, if you do not help yourself improve and accept things as they are, nobody else can help you in that aspect. It is also important that you always remember the mistakes you have done in the past and take action from it instead of regressing and going back the other way. Do not forget that mistakes are what shapes a person and sometimes, they can be inevitable. One can always learn something from a mistake and when he does, he commits never to make the same action again. However, you must also remember that a person learns and improves. You cannot always say that it is unavoidable to make a mistake because it can be when it happens repeatedly. Making the same mistakes over again is a sign that you are not doing anything to help yourself improve and move a notch higher in terms of spiritual empowerment. Become your own coach you are the only person who can always accompany yourself and check for any mistakes that you might commit. You are also the only person who can bring yourself not ever to commit the same mistake again. When you go through the process of spiritual development, it is not always a guaranteed success at the start. There are many times that a person will fail but it is in getting back up that he gets courage and determination to with standwhatever situation he has to face in the future. If you are on this journey, it is very important to have the will to achieve your goal of being independent, free, and empowered as well.

It takes a little hard work to achieve this as well as some patience. Even though the path you will be taking will have some bumps ahead, you must bear in mind that everything will end soon enough and if you focus your mind to it, you should not notice that you have already reached your goal. It is then important that each time you fail and make a mistake; you learn to accept that you also have some limitations in you. You cannot be perfect but you are trying to be the best that you can be. When you make mistakes, which are often inevitable at the start, it is normal to feel sad and a little depressed. However, this failure should not be a reason for you to sulk and even regress and go back to your old ways. Instead, you should use it as a stepping-stone so that you can move on further to your spiritual goal. When you become successful in this journey, it should feel very pleasant and light. You have reached your goal because of all your hard work and your determination. Courage is also important so that you can bravely face your shortcomings and learn to accept it. Flaws are a part of who a person is and it cannot be avoided that he has one however, it should not be a hindrance as to why he/she could not move on to his/her goal. When we try to achieve spiritual empowerment, it can be hard to go against all the temptations in the world. It can be hard to avoid indulging ourselves with what money has to offer. As they say, money makes the world go round and many times, we would forget that there are other forms of happiness in the world that no amount of money can buy. However, this is not the case for spiritual people.

A spiritual person is more aware of himself or herself. The person is more aware of his surroundings and to the sufferings of the people. This is the reason why many of them are not after material richness. These types of people find more happiness and fulfillment in the little joys of life that money is not able to bring. Thus, they are able to have a different view and concept about money, what it can do to our lives and to the people surrounding us as well. You already know that spiritual empowerment and enrichment is what you want to achieve. When you start to think of it as something that is already in you, you also start to act as if you already have that empowerment. Thus, your actions will help you work out what you need to do as things follow. Later on, you will never notice, that you have already reached what you want to achieve and you let go of the other things that is stopping you from achieving it. Remember this, When you are in your journey for spiritual enlightenment, it is important that if you feel and start to act the way an enlightened person should, you would also keep out any negative vibes. Because what you think would attract the energy around you, it is best to keep out negative thoughts from your mind to keep out negative energy as well. The Law of Attraction has been found with many uses, including in the aspect of becoming rich. According to this law, your thoughts have an energy that can attract other circumstances in life. Although this has been dismissed as a part of pseudoscience, there are still many instances in our lives where we believe that the Law of Attraction takes place.

The Law of Attraction says that if a person thinks of a specific goal in mind, feels, and knows as if it is already a truth, then things will start to follow and the universe will seem to conspire to make it a reality. Many people believe that when they start to do the same in their want to become rich, they also become one. Of course, this event does not happen instantly. When you start to think that you are already rich, or are becoming one, your actions start to modify as well. You unconsciously do things that could actually make you rich and succeed in it which is why so many of us think that the whole world willed for it to become true when the truth is, it was actually more because of our own doings. Being spiritually empowered brings us not only to awareness of ourselves but also of others and our surroundings as well. However, there are times when these concepts could clash, which is a reason why balance must be maintained between the two. That's all fine and dandy, but what about having to find someone that equally acceptable? Lets' talk about it. It is said that "godliness is a virtue, " which would make a godly person a 'virtuous' person. That makes it attractive, or creates a powerful incentive to search for someone who would be a 'virtuous' date in the religious arena. The first and most obvious religious place thought about to find a religious-minded date is undoubtedly the church. Looking for a date among your church congregation makes sense on many levels because there are several advantages to consider.

Among the most obvious advantage is that as a member or a regular attendant at the church, you have some familiarity with others who attend the church. The congregation of the church is somewhat like a family and so there is a certain level of understanding that exists among everyone. That basic level of familiarity makes it easier to feel comfortable to go on a date with someone because the person will not be a total stranger. Even if it's a situation where you don't know and never met the person at any time while you attended church, it's likely that there is another church member who you could ask about your potential date. Dating an individual from church therefore means there is a strong chance you can get a reference about the potential date, so that you would have some advance knowledge before you go on an actual date. Dating someone who is religious-minded like yourself means your date will likely have certain qualities. You can safely assume that religion and being spiritual will be important to your potential date, as those qualities are to you. And if the person is religious and spiritual, then he or she also should possess other appealing qualities such as being honest, genuine, and have a positive outlook from life. When you decide to go on dates, it means that you and the other person have an initial attraction to each other and want to find out if there are other qualities you both possess that will make the two of you good partners for a possible future life together.

Let's be reminded that spiritually is totally different from religious-minded stamina. Research has been able to show without a doubt that there is an unprejudiced analysis of the phenomenon of sex that clearly affect an individual in ways that are radically different from other basic instincts such as thirst,, hunger, pain, stress and any other feeling a normal human will endure. Commonly viewed as being a mystery and unique in itself, the individual is affected in ways that are often incomprehensible, when the charm of the other sex, is seen through the bodily sexual desire or sexual lust. This is usually portrayed in the simplest form of the male's attitude towards it, as it is of incomparable greater moral significance than the attitude to the other bodily appetites. Most males almost demand immediate satisfaction in this area whenever and wherever it seems to take control and dominate their thoughts. Apart from the obvious depths from the connection the sexual act can bring, the uniqueness of its intimacy is one of the more strongly favored responses to expect. The intimacy derived from the sex act is mostly what the female counter part is looking for through the connection. However with women and men now more commonly looking upon the sexual act as a mere exercise to create release from the stresses of the real world, even for a few minutes, the intimacy element is no longer really sought after in most encounters. Most participants still seek to have some level of heath and safely issues addressed, before indulging in the freedom of the sexual act, as without the proper precautions taken it is very possible that the act of sexual intercourse can come with a whole other set of problems both mental and physical.

When it comes to the issue of physical sexuality, women are more vulnerable that men, as there are usually a lot of underlying connective issues that affect a woman in this area rather than a man. Women are usually affected both mentally and physically in all sexual issues. The actual act of sexual intercourse more often than not has a rather significant impact on the woman in general thus creating a need to be more delicate in handling issues connected to the sexual encounter. A sexual problem can be anything that interferes with a woman natural satisfaction gained from the sexual encounter which could range from mental to physical; however in most cases it is usually noted to be of the physical nature. Ideally women should be able to enjoy a few different phases of the sexual act before and during the eventual intercourse, and this should include the stages of desire, arousal, orgasm and resolution. However, most women are unable to focus on these very important phases, which are pivotal to the success of the sexual act, because there are usually other distracting elements present. For the male, the testosterone levels usually dictate the sexual appetite of the individual, and when this is not in favorable balance, the individual will usually encounter phases of either total disinterest in sex or complete inability to perform the sexual act even when initiated. The lack of certain hormones within the body system can create the imbalance that results in the lack of sexual desire. Medical conditions are another probable contributor to the disinterest or temporary physical sexual issues. Sometimes even the medications prescribed can be a negative contributing factor to this particular part of the individual's life.

Other concerns that can affect the male's ability to successfully engage in some level of sexual activity could also stem from the inability to control premature ejaculation. This is often quite an embarrassing situation for the male to bear, thus creating the mindset that is weary of engaging in any normal healthy form of sexual activity. There is also the worry of inhibited ejaculation to deal with for some males and this is equally damaging to the male ego. This condition also further discourages the male from engaging in normal healthy sexual behavior. There are also sometimes other painful consequences to sexual encounters that force the male to avoid any form of sex. All these contribute to the negative mindset of the male thus directly impacting the physical capabilities of the individual. When this happens the males usually resort of unhealthy ways to release their built up sex drives or become totally put off with sex altogether. Sexual difficulties sometimes begin with unpleasant or traumatic encounters at some point of the past in the individual's life. When these encounters are not properly addressed they could eventually snowball into a situation where the individual is so affected by the past he or she is unable to function normally or respond normally to a sexual encounter. Some of the more common contributing factors would include marital or relationship problems, physiological problems within the individual itself, lack of trust for each other within the relationship, communication problems which could also contribute to the inability for the person to express his or her sexual preference within the sexual act itself or the phase before the actual intercourse takes place, and also any previous traumatic experiences that was not properly dealt with.

Other emotional issues that could impact the sex life of an individual would also include the state of the mind of the person which could be in a depressive mode. When depression set in, the individual would not only be an unlikely candidate for a sexual encounter but could also cause the encounter to take an unpleasant turn which could result in injury to both parties. Neglecting each other is one of the most common by products of letting issues go untreated. This is a good indication to the each other, that there is no longer an interest in keeping the relationship strong and healthy as not wanting to face issues pertaining to the relationship depicts. Depriving each other is also another unhealthy way of creating discord within the relationship. When issues are not addressed adequately, the probability of the parties within the relationship feeling that they are being taken for granted would be very high indeed. This will then create the mindset of trying to make the other party "pay" thus encouraging the negative attitude of deprivation. Dishonesty and betrayal is another product of issues surrounding the relationship not being adequately and seriously addressed. When either party feels that their feelings are not being seriously considered, then they would more likely seek comfort with someone else thus jeopardizing the future of the existing relationship. This is often the most common way that most partners use to get attention or to seek solace. Attacking each other within the boundaries of the relationship will eventually cause the relationship to fail. This is usually another method of venting frustration when the basic issues are not being addressed, thus leaving the parties no choice but to vent their frustrations on each other.

Trying to contribute equally to the marriage arrangement or relationship is important as both parties should understand that there is a part for each person within the marriage platform that should be taken seriously and without reservation. The equality factor will greatly help to determine the commitment levels each individual is willing to contribute to the relationship in order to make sure it has a fighting chance of survival. There are many ways to ensure both parties stay participative in the marriage arrangement and this would include being able to share all things, communicating well, being understanding and sensitive to each other's feelings and needs and many other positive contributing elements that will benefit the strength of the relationship. Sometimes when things don't go as well as intended, there may be a need to seek outside help to get things back on the positive track. This help may include to assistance of a councilor, a marriage therapist or any other notable person whose main function is to get the couple back into the mode where some positive progress can be made. Sex is also another important part of a successful marriage, and couple should understand the need to ensure this part of the marriage get the adequate amount of attention it needs. For most people today the idea of setting up a date night can be viewed as quite exciting and interesting. However sadly most married couples don't understand the importance and significance, of this practice, as being part of keeping the marriage fresh and exciting.

It should be explored as an activity that would further enhance the marriage and create a lasting relation that is both healthy and successful. There are several reasons as to why sex seems to play such a pivotal role within the marriage relationship and for those who are interested in maintaining the "spark" some serious thought should be given to exploring the benefits of great sex and its impact on the marriage arrangement. Sexual intercourse helps to burn calories. Though most people may think of sex as a funny way to burn calories especially when the gym is more often the place where the calorie busters are usually associated with this need, sex is also know to be able to produce similar results and is a more natural way of getting and staying nimble and in shape. Another benefit of a great sex life within the marriage is that it keeps the couple closer and more intimate thus creating an ideal and warm family unit that is both conducive and comfortable to all who are part of the family unit. Great sex does teach each party to be giving and less selfish and this extends into other parts of the couple life too, where they are more willing to have the give and take attitude as opposed to always taking or expecting to be on the receiving end. Besides this it also helps the individual to have a more complete and healthy body and mind condition. Having frequent sex is good for the heart and lowers the stress levels of anyone, thus the need to consider this as an ideal way to relieve stress. Sex for better or worse has always been a focal point in most peoples' lives, thus being able to enjoy a great sex life within a marriage if often the basis of a good and strong relationship.

If you watch the movies, especially those romantic ones, you'll start believing that sex should last the entire day, or maybe even the entire weekend. And, if you ask many women how long sex should last, you may also get similar, romanticized responses as portrayed in the movies.Yet, in reality, even good sex lasts around 30 minutes, give or take another 5-to-10 minutes. And, many women will agree that sex should realistically last about that long. Of course, that does not mean that you shouldn't plan for an all-day, or even an all-weekend "hot and passionate" adventure, every now and then. (Yes, just like in the movies.) But, as far as the rest of the sexual encounters is concerned, nobody wants every single session to last longer than 30 to 40 minutes. Not even women, if they're being completely honest. (They do have other things to do, you know?) So, for starters, let the above realization sink in and relieve some of the "performance pressure" from your mind. Certain sexual positions can help you to last longer in the bedroom simply because the penis is not being stimulated as much. Obviously, less direct penis stimulation would result in longer performance time, for you. One of the best positions for this purpose is when the woman is on top, in the sitting or straddling position. This one works best if you are laying down flat, versus sitting on a chair or the edge of the bed. She can be sitting on top of you.And, of course, you'll want to ask her to go slowly when she's on top. Because, vigorous hard-and-fast thrusting will naturally create a lot more friction...and it will also turn your mind on much more...both of which can cause you to climax much sooner.

Chapter Eleven: Warm Attention

It can also help if you aren't looking directly at her the entire time. That way, she can be less self-conscious and let go, and be able to enjoy herself a lot more (which would come in handy for you, later on.) Feel free to gently run your palms up and down her body, grab and caress her breasts, and so on to keep the interaction alive, even if your eyes are closed at times. This one is a no-brainer, really. Yet, for some reason, men either forget about it in the heat of passion, or they simply ignore it. The easiest "instant fix" to lasting longer is to focus on her and let her finish first. Don't rush this one. And, especially don't rush her. That's a common mistake most guys make. Give her body and her lots of attention. Get her warmed up and purring, with lots of attention and foreplay. And keep her guessing keep her on her toes. That means, instead of starting at the top (kissing her lips) and gradually moving down - in a straight and predictable line, move around a bit. Move back and forth, between different hot spots on her body, so she's not expecting your every move. (If she's able to see what's coming next, it will get boring for her. It will also resemble exactly what every other guy has done for her. So, be different.) The important thing here is, by focusing on giving her pleasure first, it takes the pressure off of you...especially if you have a tendency to climax too quickly. That absence of mental pressure will automatically allow your mind (and body) to last longer, without your trying to do so.

Finally, and most importantly do not make it your unfaltering mission to give her an orgasm. As mentioned above, don't rush it and don't rush her unless she clearly wants you to. If your main focus is on getting her to climax, she will sense it very easily. And, it will put unnecessary pressure on her to "get there." That will only make it harder for her to have an orgasm. So, just enjoy her body and her presence. When you are relaxed, she will be able to relax as well. And, that will help both of you to enjoy the experience and the happy endings that naturally follow. Of course, after she has enjoyed at least one explosion of pleasure, it won't matter how long it takes you to get to yours. Instead, focus on what's going on right now - in front of you. Focus on the present moment. Primarily, that would include focusing on her and on all the little pleasures you and she are sharing with each other... whatever that may be at any given moment whether it's kissing her lips and feeling hers against yours, feeling her body rubbing against yours, or whatever is happening at that moment. Continue to focus on what's right in front of you as each moment unfolds. And, you will find that your mind starts to relax...it stops thinking, worrying, or even fearing about climaxing too early. Doing the above will also help you to experience pleasure all over your body, instead of intensifying it only around your genital area. And, that's a giant plus in helping you to last much longer. The next "quick fix" solution to lasting longer in bed is to simply ignore the early finish (or even arrange a planned execution, beforehand.)

In other words, you can just enjoy your time with your partner. And if you happen to climax too early, simply shrug it off and get back to focusing on her, and on giving her more pleasure. (If you make a big deal out of climaxing too soon, she will too.) Also, she won't mind your coming too early, unless you immediately roll over and pass out. So, if you do happen to finish early, no problem. Now, start focusing on her, and help her get close to reaching the climax point...or even finishing. And, you may often find that by focusing on her for a while, you will become ready again for a second round. Remember, don't try to force yourself to get ready for another round. Just enjoy your time with her, and allow your body to do what it does, naturally. (Get your mind, and mental pressure, out of the equation.) By the way, if you do find yourself becoming ready for an encore performance, you may also realize that you will usually last much longer on the second round. Another quick and easy way to slow things down a bit, if you feel an explosion about to happen, is to stop for a moment and press just below the head of your penis. You can use two fingers in a clamping motion (one on top and one below) to squeeze this area, mainly the part on the underside of your penis. Doing the above technique can slow down the blood pumping into your penis, and can help to temporarily delay your release. When you feel things slowing down, you can get back to doing what you were and buy yourself some additional minutes.

Of course, if you decide to use this technique again, when you feel another build up happening, you can. That should give you a few more minutes, or maybe more. Here's a bonus tip which isn't an "instant" fix like the ones shared above, but it can be very helpful for you to become aware of. As touched on earlier, finishing early is often due to what's going on in your mind mainly because most men have "trained" their own minds and bodies to get there faster without realizing what the overall consequences would be (like, when they're with a partner.) The good news is, you can retrain your body (and mind) to slow down and not rush to the finish line. From here on out, if you find yourself masturbating, first of all become aware of your automatic tendency to want to finish quickly. And, also become aware of where your default "finish line" is, how long it currently takes you to finish. Next, purposely slow yourself down. Take your time and make the event last for as long as you can, instead of rushing to finish. Try to add up to five more minutes to your time. And, if you find yourself coming close to climaxing, back off...stop, and slow things down as close to the main event as possible. (If you're not able to, try again next time, and stop a second or two sooner than the previous time.) So, as you start to get close to climaxing, stop and give your body a short break and take some long, deep breaths to calm things down a bit.

Then, start over and get back up as close to the finish line as possible.Try to repeat the above process up to three times, if you can. With practice, you may be able to add another 10 to 15 minutes to your performance time. Then, when you're with a partner, you can use the same technique of slowing down or stopping for a moment, and taking a few deep breaths in, before continuing. And, yes, you can even repeat the process a few times, when you're with a partner, just as you practiced on your own. The most important thing for you to realize here is, finishing too early is not that big of a deal. It happens to many men, including the so-called "stallions."When you understand that, the mental shift in your mind alone will often help to have it occur less frequently for you... or it may even stop happening completely. And, if it does happen, I've given you a number of "instant" ways above, to improve your performance time, as well as turn any unforeseen incidents to your advantage. It is sometime necessary to be able to read into the body language of the other party to better understand what is going on and how to best deal with any surfacing situation. Learning how to read the various body language signs will also allow each party to better understand and interpret the partner's wants and needs and work accordingly to accommodate them as far as possible. The following are some popular body language signs that can be used to tip off the other party as to the current mindset and general disposition of each other.

Eyes clamped shut, stiffness in the neck and shoulders generally depict an individual who is either upset or not really happy with something. These signals can be used to effectively help to defuse any situation before it goes out of hand and to also help to divert the person's attention to something that is more pleasurable and less upsetting. This often takes the individual experiencing negativity away from the offending situation and thus encouraging a better frame of mind. It should be noted that not all body language signals are negative. When an individual is in a sexy mood there are also some subtle and not so subtle body language moves that will allow the other party to respond accordingly should they wish to. This is important to learn as it will help bring the couple closer when such displays of body language attempts are well read and acted upon. In most cases when the response is favorable, the party using the body language skills to communicate will be so encouraged and happy, that they would in all likelihood make it worthwhile and pleasurable for the responding party. This of course will heighten the communication mode to a more deeper and fulfilling experience. Understanding that listening is anything but a passive activity is a good place to start. Neither is listening expected to be an activity that is neutral and nothing else. In fact good listeners are able to come up with good workable solutions as they are able to understand and follow the various contributing factors to any particular situation being discussed.

Developing the skill of being able to listen carefully also allows the individual to "hear" things that are not really being verbalized and yet important enough to need attention. Sometimes these unspoken bits of information can be more informative than what is actually being said through the conversation, and when these bits of information allow the listen to act in a manner that is both soothing and helpful to the speaker, a huge amount of positive effects can be experienced. Good listeners are usually people who are able to eventually become wise people. Listening takes a certain level of restraint and thus allows the person to mull over the matter being verbalized before making any judgment calls or giving any response. By simply listening, the person is actually allowing the other party to vent everything and anything until fully satisfied. After this happens the person will then be more receptive to any advice or comments made, thus allowing for some type of solution to be made. Two people taking and trying to get the thoughts and views across will not in any way help an already delicate situation. Most humans need to be touched especially within the perimeters of a healthy and happy relationship. Without the important touching factor constantly being exercised, both parties will eventually feel the missing ingredient and this could lead to some detrimental results. Touching and being touched is something every healthy relationship should experience daily and as frequently as possible. The need for touch is very primal and basic, and stroking this desire will leave both parties feeling cherished and fulfilled.

It should be understood that not all touching should ideally lead to some form of sexual activity, as this is not only pressurizing but also quite unnecessary. The act of touching should primarily be exercised as way to convey love, intimacy, comfort, happiness and any other positive connotations which are healthy for relationships. A loving physical gesture can go along way and some say further than the spoken word. A lot of people respond well to the physical touch as long as there is no sexual connotation to it, unless the touch was specifically meant to be so. Most people are simply unaware of the huge effects a simple touch can convey, thus often making the serious mistake of not incorporating the touch action into the everyday lives within a relationship. Most marriages on the verge of collapse will usually concur on the fact that there was almost relatively no touching within the relationship, unless sex was the agenda. This is rather a sad scenario, to live with, as touching does say a lot about the feelings of love and closeness of the couple within the relationship. Even when having a simple conversation with the other party, some touching could be initiated to help the person relax and be more receptive to what is being said. Committing to good communication will also allow the couple to resolve issues before they become out of control problems. Good communication skill will allow both parties to put forth their individual views without resorting to under handed measures such as insults and other negative verbal expressions.

Being able to fine tune the art of mutually beneficial conversation will certainly help prepare the couple for times when confrontations surface, as the previous ability to converse well, will help to keep both of them focused on resolving the matter in the most amicable way. Committing to good communication will also help both parties to explore and find suitable solutions as quickly as possible rather than lingering on the problem. In doing so the problem can be contained and there is less chances of it escalating and taking over the lives of both parties. Can you use your spirituality to escape from your problems in life? Yes! It is possible. If you have problems in life, it doesn't mean that your life is meaningless. Remember that there is always a solution for every problem. Man is a complex compound. He is made up of one part mind and one part matter. When the two parts are harmoniously joined, he sparkles like a diamond with the joy of life. But when the two parts conflict or are unbalanced, the result is a dismal lump of coal. We tend to forget that we are not physical beings having a spiritual experience, but spiritual beings undergoing a physical experience. The spiritual being needs the human body to explore life to the fullest and to propagate life on earth. And the material body seeks the spirit to motivate it higher, beyond the baser instincts of animals. A balance has to be struck between our physicality and our spirituality. There are many ways and aspects to this quest. Sexuality ponders on Sex & the Spirit. And finally we close with a few reflections on the power of prayer.

To achieve a balanced mind and in turn to live a balanced physical existence, three qualities have to be in perfect equilibrium – Wisdom, Benevolence and Courage. A balance of these 3 qualities ensures that you achieve your goals in life with zest and discipline while also being compassionate to your fellow beings, guided by wisdom. If you only have passion without wisdom and compassion, you may become a cruel and foolish person. Benevolence alone without willpower and wisdom will make you a useless romantic idealist. And wisdom alone without action and kindness will turn you into a reclusive hermit. Theosophy teaches that when these three virtues are kept in equilibrium, Man can become fully effective and happy in the world. Just try it out. Make a list of your friends and tick away in 3 columns against their names. You will be able to see one or two of the above qualities missing in them. And you will find that he or she who has all the three virtues in balance is the best human being among them all. Imagine you are walking down the street. There"s a stranger standing by the street side. A girl walks looking backwards, bumps into a fat man, and gets the wind knocked out of her. You laugh heartily and so does the stranger near you. You look at each other and smile in acknowledgement. You don"t know each other, but the joke created a brief cheery connection between the two of you. Sometimes your spirit becomes so lost and distant from your physical self, that it takes a good bout of laughter to get back in touch.

Chapter Twelve: Spiritual Balance

Your spirit is a funny guy too. Why do we have to look at all things spiritual as solemn quests for enlightenment? Spirits don't wear long hooded robes and carry candles in dark dungeons. Nor do they prefer to freeze on top of the Himalayas with half naked hermits for company. Our spirits are the residents of our bodies. It"s just that we are so busy building better bodies and furnishing them with shiny things that we end up evicting the lawful resident or banishing him to a dark and damp corner of our cellar. Get that spirit back up into the living hall of your life. Treat him to a drink and enjoy a good laugh. His hearty laughter will ring through the rooms of your body and resonate in your heart, lungs, veins and bones! When your Body and Spirit have found each other again through a good laugh, they can walk cheerfully through life. Laughter is your mind"s way of saying that nothing is stronger than your Soul. The day you stop smiling and laughing, your spirit languishes in that cellar again and your lonely body starts feeling cold and miserable once again. The importance of a healthy sexual balance is often ignored in the search for physical-spiritual equilibrium. One extreme sees men and women dissatisfied with their sex lives and the other end is occupied with people frantically fornicating in the search for true fulfillment. Let us explore a few thoughts on Sex and the Spirit. In these modern times where stress, career and lengthy educational years make increasing demands on people, the number of men and women with dysfunctional or totally non-existent sex lives is increasing.

If abstinence is self imposed for spiritual reasons that"s fine, but the average Joe or Jane are bound to feel frustrated and imbalanced without healthy sexual activity for years together. Repressed sexuality and childhood abuse can add on to a deadly mix resulting in sexual crimes or deviant behavior. On the other hand, promiscuous behavior carries along the pattern of unsafe sexual practices and the possible baggage of guilt and assorted negative emotions. Failed relationships fuel further exploration, leading on to a hopeless trail of divorces and zipless one-night stands. The goal in a sexual quest is that one loving man or woman who completes us both sexually and spiritually. There is nothing more satisfying than falling asleep after a session of great lovemaking with your arms around a spouse you love. That is even more satisfying when you know that the kids are happily sleeping in the next room. Sex after all was basically invented by our Creator for - procreation. While a healthy sexual relationship strikes a great balance for a couple, the weighing scale itself turns to gold when children enter their lives. Creativity and a passionate sexuality tuned to each other"s needs can keep a marriage hot for decades. A zest for life leads to healthy sex and vice versa. A husband and wife can become each other"s yin and yang, thus striking a delightful balance between themselves as well as their individual mind, body and soul. Prayer is defined as the act of addressing a god or spirit with the intention of asking for something or just worshipping and giving praise to the deity.

Scientific studies often explore the ability of prayer to heal the sick and injured. But every evening when we get down to pray, it is we who heal ourselves, bringing our mind, body and soul to an intimate get together. Some African societies still practice Animism, a tradition wherein plants, rocks, waterfalls and even natural phenomena like rain and thunder are believed to embody divinity. Connecting with spirits is still a strong part of animism today. A shaman listens to these spirits and conveys the messages to his people. In modern times, an individual has to function as his own personal shaman. The Mind prays to the Soul to heal the Body. In these stressful times, the spiritual and physical selves get alienated and sometimes are not even on speaking terms! In the words of William Inge – " Prayer gives a man the opportunity of getting to know a gentleman he hardly ever meets. I do not mean his maker, but himself." Praying is also used as a faith healing process to prevent or cure illness. While the efficacy of faith healing is looked at with skepticism by the scientific community, both eastern and western science accepts the ability of prayer and meditation to bring about peace in an individual. Whereas community prayer and ritualized religion requires the devotees to use pre-scripted prayers, each individual can also use his own inner dialogue when he meditates alone. Either way can be quite effective to harmonize the body and soul of the truly devout.

Oriental culture is rich in spiritual philosophy and practice. Numerous martial arts and meditation techniques have explored the relation between the body and mind for ages. You don"t need any kind of expensive equipment or facilities to practice yoga. All you need to bring to the practice is your mind, body and spirit" along with loads of discipline and a strong desire to achieve a physical-spiritual balance. Have you forgotten to feed your soul as much as you nourish your body? Do something that gives you an inner pleasure. Take a quiet walk in a park and listen to the birds. Go for a swim. Read a classic work of literature. Listen to a melodious song. Even if you are in the middle of the maddening office, close your eyes and visualize an oasis of greenery and water deep inside your mind. Walk deep into your soul and wash your face with the sparkling waters of that oasis. When you open your eyes again, you will be fresh and balanced and can tackle work again. Thus your soul has uplifted your fatigued body. You can practice yoga or transcendental meditation or play a tennis game or just walk briskly down the stairs instead of taking the elevator. The heady rush of endorphins brought on by exercise is your body"s reward for the effort. Your rejuvenated body will lift your tired soul. The body and soul can work together like this, each taking turns to cheer up the other. You know that your inner soul always loves your physical body and is always ready to help. But it is often the body that forgets the soul, turns down its advice and suffers as a result. When your body and spirit join forces, nothing can stop you!

The best way to recharge your soul is by giving love to other beings, be they human, animal or even plant life. As you give, your love awakens the love within other beings. If you hate, the same negative energy is reciprocated. He is truly great who gives love to the one who spews hate. The word balance is crucial. Getting too caught up with spirituality is as dangerous as obsessing with your body. You are your best teacher. Look within and look without. Your inner soul and the outer world are like yin and yang, always circling and affecting each other. For centuries, spiritual precepts have pointed us to the heart and soul as the source of wisdom, truth, peace, and eternal life. We call it the heart Andy soul because these deeper realities are felt most strongly in the region of the physical heart. But, the spiritual heart and soul isn't limited to a location in your body. The heart and soul is the totality of your connection with the crucial qualities and greater dimensions of your true nature as limitless existence. Any full exploration of the bigger truth of your existence must include a discovery of the capabilities and qualities of this tender, loving, and wise aspect of your true nature is a pointing beyond the experience of the Heart and its wisdom, peace, and love to the possibility of acknowledging these essential qualities as who and what you are. The heart and soul with all its joy, satisfaction, peace, love, and wisdom isn't simply something you may experience more totally it's what you've always been and always will be.

A lot of beliefs and suppositions shape and limit our experience of life connecting and the sense of our self even when we're not consciously considering them. They're thoughts and concepts that are so deeply trusted that they're not even questioned, like "life is short" or "I have to have more money." Moreover, these notions and assumptions render other thoughts, which add to the momentum of thinking and keep your heart and soul, the sensation of your self, little and compressed. Beliefs strongly shape the experience of your world. The first is the belief in a management to your life. Commonly this management is towards more, dissimilar, or better experiences; but occasionally it's framed in contrary terms as not less, equal, or not sorrier. In either event, there's a profoundly held notion that life ought to move or shift in a specific way. Naturally, things do shift, which keeps the hope alive that they'll change in the way you wish them to. This profoundly held assumption that matters may or ought to be better connotes a little you. The directivity of this assumption is based on a point of reference: matters ought to be better for you. If matters ought to be better for you, then you have to be lacking something. This supposition and the thinking it returns help maintain a little, compressed sense of your world as that's the implied point of reference of the presumption.

Chapter Thirteen: Drift of Love

A compressed sense of self is the presumption that physical experience is the most genuine. This is such a widely held supposition that any other predilection may get you pronounced demented.Even really sensitive and spiritually-oriented individuals who have had really true and profound experiences of additional dimensions are frequently pulled by this premise back toward the physical into a more confined experience of reality. There are a lot of dimensions to truth besides the strictly physical, and as a human, your experience admits all of these dimensions. There are the dimensions of ideas, emotion, and hunch. And on the far side of those, are dimensions of complete presence. A lot of these dimensions are more actual than even physical truth. Experiences of this surpassing reality provide a surpassing sense of your self that's much broader and more perfect than the strictly physical sense of your self. This limitation may impact each experience you get. By centering on how it's going for your core of reality, you may miss some of the richest most fundamental possibilities in life. The largest truths might not even be particularly well-situated for your core of reality. Profound states of love and blissfulness may be wearing from a purely physical position. Inquiring what you may do about this limitation will only reward it. A different hypothesis is to explore the sense of restriction that identification with the core of reality gives to your awareness and your heart and soul.

Anything you or anybody else has ever accomplished has been the drive of love. What shapes this drift of love is the sense of me. What we're forever doing is attending of the self, whether it's a little sense of self or a more extended one. If that sense of self is compressed and small, we mind that me. And when it's enlarged, we mind that bigger sense of self. All we have ever executed is to take care of the self in the best way we understand how, which is always a loving act. However, naturally, when our actions solely take care of a constricted me, they don't take care of or allow for other things. For instance, we may take care of our taste-buds, but not our entire body. Or if we're so identified with a notion that all we may do is see it, we might not be minding our entire existence. Taking care of only the taste-buds or only the emotions is yet a loving act, but because it's such a narrow-minded way of loving ourselves, it may be neglectful or even adverse to other aspects of our existence. It's possible to realize the love that's already inside of us and already working through all of us. It's in realizing that love that the possibility exists for even better recognition of love. On the contrary, when we decline any aspect of love which includes anything that's occurring the more constricted our experience will be Andy the less totally loving our actions will be. So, in condemning, we in reality become more like what we condemn.

Being is taking care of self and connecting with a higher power. This leads to a gratitude of everything you do and everything that happens an appreciation of the way existence moves each time it moves. Love pd pouring out everyplace. There's no evidence of the lack of love. What a surprise to find this in a domain that appears so full of issues and matters that need to be changed. In this culture where more is felt to be greater, there's frequently an implication that greater truths are better. If your heart and soul can open and enlarge, then it might seem best to find a way to open it all the way and keep it that way. If your gist is forever connected to a higher power and accurately, appropriately opening or contracting to show you how real each moment's perspective is, then the best outcome of experiencing a small truth is for your heart and soul to contract and show you how little that truth is. There's never a need to have a greater or smaller experience, as existence still existence even in the little experiences. Its nature is the same, and part of its nature is this capability to separate how true how complete a specific perspective is. True freedom is when you may move in and out of recognition with a small sense of your world. You don't need to take my word for it. Discover what occurs in your heart and soul if you simply let the opening and closing of your sense of self be merely the way it is today.

Perhaps you may rest now from the dream of experiencing and having everything. Make acquaintances with the angels, who while invisible are forever with you. Frequently call them, and make great use of their help and assistance in all your temporal and spiritual matters. We're forever in the company of angels whether we decide to acknowledge them or not. They're forever by your side, guiding and protecting you whether you decide to believe in them or not. Connecting with your angels may be a very rewarding and spiritually fulfilling experience. I'll demonstrate you how you may become closer with your angels, associate with them and gain knowledge, insight, protection, guidance and/or emotional solace from that association. Connecting with your angels is truly very easy. Your angels love to celebrate each moment that you're making a conscious attempt to connect with them. They wish you to call on them for any reason or state of affairs, even if it seems little to you. They welcome the chance to prove their existence to you, again and again. Begin now to build a growing relationship with your angels(or any of your spiritual guides and assistants) and observe your lifebecome better in each way and you'll see the wonders and miracles blossom. Perhaps the experience of eternal life and connection with other than temporal things doesn't need to be captured. This is something we may also unfold gradually in stages like a meal or novel that we slowly savor instead of rush through.

We are and always have been recognizing the truth even when we experience only a little part of it. The fullness of existence is likewise revealed in the small truths that comprise our lives. Existence is never harmed by the limited perspectives we go through. Being isn't dependent on any specific way of sensing your self nor even on the absence of a sense of self. Existence is already resting inside the endless opening and closing of your heart and soul, so you may as well savor the ride. A lot of the problems we have in our relationships stem from a lack of understanding, in other words we have no idea why guys act the way they do. In fact, they often don't know why they act the way they do so it's no surprise we have trouble deciphering their responses. However, before we begin to explore these fundamental differences, it's worth taking a step back and looking at ourselves in the mirror because if we don't learn to finally accept who and what we are, we will never be able to make the necessary changes to become the woman men adore. The biggest problem we have right now is our perception of ourselves. Women's lib has been taken to a whole new level and from simply meaning that women should have equal rights to men in society, it has come to mean that women should not be women and they should act more like men. The reason for this is quite simple. Men are competitive by nature, women are not.

Therefore, to succeed in the workplace, more and more women have had to become just as competitive as men and in many cases more so because they start out with a handicap in the eyes of the competition. They are women. Unfortunately, though, many women have taken this competition to a whole new level and their drive to succeed has convinced them that being a woman means being weak, so they have to shut off their feelings and act more like the guys they work with. Sadly women are grossly mistaken because our femininity is in no way a weakness, but, in fact, a strength, as it is the one thing that allows us to influence men much more effectively than any argument or competition ever will. Men are disarmed by a woman's softness simply because men were designed to fight and women were designed to nurture. Men are goal driven and they feel good about themselves when they manage to achieve their goals because they prove that they are worthy and competent. If they do so on their own then that is an even greater testament to their power and strength. Because men are hardwired to solve their problems on their own they rarely talk about them. When they do, it means they need advice and help. If women can understand this side of men, then they will understand why men hate being corrected or advised without asking for it. It makes them feel incompetent and they feel that you don't trust them to solve the problem.

This is also why men tend to offer solutions when women talk to them about their problems. It is because if another man were to share his problems, it is an unspoken request for help so he feels honored to provide a solution. When he provides a solution for the woman he loves, it is an expression of his love but when a woman gets upset because she perceives that he isn't listening or emphasizing he has no idea what he did to upset her. The result is that he withdraws and basically blocks her out. Sex is a vital part of any relationship and it can make or break an otherwise wonderful couple. The biggest problem women have when it comes to sex is that they tend to be overly self conscious. This then leads on a lack of focus on what is going on and you tend to be so worried about how you look that you forget to enjoy what's happening. Not only that, but some women also voice their insecurities which makes it even worse. Ladies, you need to stop focusing on what you think is wrong with you and enjoy the moment. If he's there with you and he is telling you that you turn him on then believe him. After all, guys can't fake it. Seriously, they can't. If he's in the bedroom with you, then he's already turned on by who you are right now. Pointing out your cellulite or trying to hide a part of your body for fear you might look fat or wobbly is like shining a spotlight on it for him to see, where he probably would never have noticed otherwise.

Men just don't see those things we think of as imperfections until you point them out. Another problem many relationships run into is that sex becomes routine and then slowly dries up and disappears completely. Society is as much to blame for this as we are. We forget that sex is supposed to be fun as well as a great way to bond with your partner. However, they were still deeply in love with each other and it showed because they expressed themselves. In other words, variety is the spice of life and sex is nothing to be ashamed of. The more variety you have in your sex life, the less likely it is that it will become boring and a matter of obligation rather than enjoyment. There are so many things you can do to keep your sex life interesting, from surprising your man with an impromptu romp to role playing for him, you can be sure he will definitely want to play along. Remember that it doesn't always have to be a Hollywood production of the perfect romantic evening. Sometimes a hot, sweaty, fast roll in the hay is exactly what the doctor ordered. You'll also find that it is a great way to relieve tension as well. However, don't expect to share a wonderful talk afterwards and then get upset when he falls asleep. Men are hard pressed to share their feelings at any time, let alone after a good round of sex when their brain has completely switched off. Seniors are often looked over in this area,when it comes to sex, pleasure and spirituality. Older people know how to read some easily by their actions and what they say. This is because they have had plenty experience dating in their past.

Chapter Fourteen: Dating Basics

In order to go out on a proper date, you must know the mature dating basics before going. You don't want to embarrass yourself or do something that is frowned upon during a date. Two adults should always be upfront about what they want and this way they can communicate better. If one adult has a different desire in a relationship, it probably won't work out. The other person is looking to get married within a few months and settle a family. This is all too much for the person who just wants a casual relationship. They draw back because they are afraid of getting hurt or sucked into a place where they won't be able to enjoy the opposite sex. Most adults know that it is important to meet in safe places, otherwise if something goes wrong no one would be there to save them. This is very true if you are woman but keep in mind, it can also be dangerous for men as well. If you are participating in online dating, you always need to be extra careful. You should at least know the person's first and last name before going on a date, a few things about their life, plus their living situation. Meeting up with anyone in a short amount of time is dangerous and you will look desperate. Try to take things slowly, even if you are dating multiple people. You want to be sure the other person is interested in you. Now, if you are a woman - you don't have to tell your age. Some woman look very young but are ashamed of their age and don't want to appear too old.

Men don't have a problem with this but sometimes they may hesitate if the woman is not mature enough for them. Other women enjoy dating men that are younger than them because of the sex appeal or they may just like them for their personality. There are plenty of situations that go on in developing relationships. If you are in your early thirties or forties, please don't sign up for a senior dating site. These sites are usually reserved for people fifty and up who are looking for someone to spend the rest of their life with. A huge age gap isn't a good idea and your differences could damage the relationship. However, there are some people who do have gaps in age and get along just fine. Just be wary of senior dating sites. Instead, sign up for regular dating sites that allow users from 18 and up to date. You will find plenty of people who are older since there is no max age. On top of that, most of these sites allow you to look for a person based on the age. Choosing someone close to your age will yield the best results and the two of you will get along just perfectly. People who are close to the same age usually have the same mentality. Being upfront about what you want is very important. You need to discuss your relationship goals with the other person. If you are not interested in your date as someone to be in a relationship with, it is a good idea to tell them. Be upfront and never lead them on. You can just tell them you aren't ready for a relationship with them or they aren't your type. Give them an honest reason.

Don't be afraid to let your date know that you don't want to be with them. It may hurt them but break it to them lightly and let them know the two of you can always be friends. Their feelings might be crushed but at least you won't have to beat around the push. They've probably faced rejection before in their lives so don't worry too much about it. Make sure you treat them as a special friend and if there is anything you can do for them, let them know. If you are upfront about what you want and your date does not try to sacrifice a few things for you, it is probably best to move on. For example, let's say your date only eats sushi and you your diet only consists of cooked meat. You may have a dispute about where to go. If they have never tried sushi, they can always give it a go just this once. This is called making a sacrifice. Remember that you can let them know there are other things on the menu they can enjoy like soups too. A person who truly is into you will do this from time to time but it is a good idea to allow them to choose some activities that they'd like to participate in as well. By protecting yourself, you won't regret anything that happens in the future. It doesn't matter if you are a man or woman either. Most say that women are the only ones that need to protect themselves since they are much smaller and less strong as me are. Men should also protect themselves and lookout for anything unusual. There have been a few instances where women go out on dates and once they get the chance, they will steal the man's wallet.

This is why it's a good idea to look up her name and background before you go on a date. This can get expensive if you are dating a few women at a time but there are sites that let you check unlimited backgrounds of certain people by paying a one0time upfront fee or going for a monthly membership. Some of the top sites include Itenlius, CorporateScreening, or BeenVerified. All of these sites are established and have different plans according to what your needs are. If you just want a criminal background check only, you can easily obtain this without paying a lot of money. There are also free trials if you want to test out a company. We recommend doing this if you are new to background checks. This will help you see the website features before you decide to purchase anything on their website. You can try them free for a couple days and then upgrade your plan. As we said earlier, age shouldn't matter when going out. Not unless you are dating someone who is 8 years older or younger than you. Obviously, you don't want to be with someone who has a huge age gap. If you are uncomfortable telling your age, just let your date know that you'll tell them later. Obviously, with online dating - you'll be able to look up someone's age through their profile. Otherwise, if you are dating someone from work or a social event, you don't have to tell them your date. Most people won't care how old you are. Their goal is to find someone who has a sense of humor, is attractive, responsible, and active.

These are the most important things in a relationship for them and if something is out of place, they won't want to continue with the relationship. You should also have high standards but make sure you aren't too picky when it comes to choosing a date. If you are a man asking a woman for her age who is obviously much older then you, she may feel slightly uncomfortable. It is always best to maintain a healthy relationship and go out on dates for a few weeks before. Always give her a compliment before you ask this sort of question, otherwise it's not advisable to ask at all. You could slyly say something like "Wow, you look very young... how old are you by the way?". A woman is more inclined to give out her age if you give her a compliment like this while asking the question. Otherwise, we recommend keeping out any age talk, especially on a first date. Having a positive attitude is a great way to start your day and even start a date. By having a positive attitude, you'll be able to create strong vibes that let the person know you able to cope with certain situations. Usually, people who have positive attitudes are able to get past events in life that can bring them into a deep depression. By staying positive, you'll be able to allow the other person to get close to you. For example, if you are walking down the street frowning - not many people will smile at you. Now, if you are walking with a grin and holding your head high, someone is most likely to smile at you. Someone who tends to "glow" is the one that other people want to be around.

By smiling at another, you are making them feel comfortable and also adding positivity to the date. All it takes is one smile to brighten someone's day. If you smile at them, they are naturally inclined to converse with you and will want to learn more. They feel you are a warm and positive person because of the smile you've flashed them. A facial expression can be quite powerful if you think about it. When going on a date, always prevent any upcoming negative thoughts. Never judge your date based on how they look, what they are wearing or what they say. People grow up around different families and some are from different cultures than us and this is why we need to understand that negative thoughts won't help us. If you judge someone right away, you'll probably have a negative thought about them. Perhaps the guy you are dating came in with blue hair. He was actually trying to dye some of his stray gray hairs but his kid's played a cruel trick on him last night. He is usually a well-shaven and clean man who doesn't do things like piercing himself in odd places or known for having any tattoos. Once he explains what happened to him, you will probably feel guilty for having such negative thoughts about his choice of hair "fashion". Always treat others as you'd want to be treated. Be positive around them and never send them any negative messages or speak in a negative tone. You want to appear calm and inviting towards people. It doesn't matter if they are a friend or a date. You should practice this so that way it will come naturally.

Being optimistic means being hopeful and confident about the future. You should look at your date and think of what wonderful things they have in store for you. If you notice some of their best qualities, focus on those instead of looking at any bad habits of theirs. They will see that you are trying to look past any negative habits they may have. Remember that it is possible for people to change. In many instances, people will change according to the crowd they are with. If they are with friends that are trouble makers or are extremely rude to people, then you would take on the same qualities. However, if you go with a church group every few days and have brunch while talking about the beauty of life - you'll begin to appreciate how lucky you are to be living. People who are optimistic are like magnets they draw others around them because of the pure energy they put out. Having positive thoughts about the future will allow you to go on a date without any anxiety. You won't have to think about "Does he like me?" or start fidgeting through the whole date because you are nervous. Think positive thoughts in your head. You could very well say to yourself "I am a wonderful person and I'm sure anyone who meets me will like me!". Get up every day and stand in the mirror. While standing in front of the mirror, give yourself positive words or a compliment. This will boost your confidence and also allow you to focus only on the positive things.

Don't ever look at your date in a negative way. If he or she is way too talkative, think of it as a good thing. If you can't get a word in, just be playful with your date and say "Hey, when do I get to talk!". They'll get the hint quickly and settle down to hear about the things you want to tell them or ask them. Senior dating sites should be avoided most of the time, especially if you are under the age of 50. People in their middle age shouldn't date seniors. Nor should 18 year olds date someone in their early thirties. It just doesn't make sense and there is a good chance that the two of you will have different morals, ethics, reasoning, and habits. You want someone who is very close to your age. Being five to eight years apart isn't a big difference though and this is generally okay. Anything over that age might be a problem in a relationship. Someone who is older is generally more experienced when it comes to people, is more responsible financially, and tends to think logically instead of with their heart. A person who is younger may behave recklessly and take life for granite. You certainly don't want to date someone like this. Another reason why you should be wary of senior dating sites is because you want to date someone who is the same age of you. Ten years apart isn't a good idea. If you end up growing extremely attached to the person and they are 10-20 years older than you, you might be very fearful of death. What if your love died of a stroke or something happened to them?

Loss of a loved one, especially a husband or wife is devastating. Do yourself a favor and think of the future before dating anyone. Most senior dating sites are only reserved for people forty five and up. If you are only forty years old, you probably won't be able to sign up for the website since there are age restrictions. Don't waste your time with that. There are plenty of sites you can visit that are only for adults. There won't be any young teens on the site. Some high school students will sign up for a dating website when it is only reserved for adults. They may even have a fake I.D to get into bars and clubs when they go on their date. Do yourself a favor and if someone contacts you who looks very young, ask them how old they are. Also, check their I.D to make sure it is legitimate before going on the date. If you believe they look way to young, use your gut instinct and don't go on the date at all. Not everyone will tell you the truth so it is very important to listen to yourself. Mixing love and money is the worst thing you can do. If you are an attractive woman who only go for men who have jobs that are over compensating, you probably only attract older men or someone who isn't as attractive as you are. These men can be incredibly sensitive and if you aren't really interested in them as a person, it will hurt them in the future. Instead of looking at someone's wallet, it is important to look at the qualities they have in a relationship. Are they sensitive? Do they treat people kindly? Are they romantic? These are a few questions most people would want to know about their date.

Men can also use women as well. They will say anything to get close to them and they know if the woman is extremely independent when it comes to having a job, they will do all they can to have her purse in their hands. If you have already been out on a few dates and are now good friends with the person you are dating, it is important that you never borrow them any money. Offering gifts is fine but money is different. If you've known them for over two years, offering money is acceptable but not someone you've been on a 5th date with. There have been many times where a woman or man borrows a substantial amount of money to someone and they skip out on the next date. If your date is buying you extravagant gifts without asking and you always take the gifts from them, it is always a good idea to give back. Get them something special once you reach your 8th date. By the 8th date, it is safe to say that they are interested in you -otherwise they would have left long ago. You don't need to buy them something expensive either. Chocolates or flowers would be perfect. A gift is to show someone you truly care about them and also it say's "I appreciate you". Many times, people who are older will often settle down because of their age. You should take time to go out on dates with many different people before deciding who is the perfect match for you. After all, this is a decision for your future. Once you find the one you want to be with, you will spend the rest of your life with them.

Chapter Fifteen: Strengthen Your Marriage

If marriage is a strong possibility or you want to have kids, you'll need to find someone who has the same morals as you and is interested in the same activities you are. Now, it is important to know that the two of you don't have to do everything together but having a few things in common is very important. Some people only agree to marriage because they are afraid they aren't getting any younger. The majority of these people end up being stuck in relationships that they really don't want to be in and about 75% of the time, it will end up in early divorce. We strongly recommend taking things slow and if the person you want to be with also has mutual feelings of taking it to the next step, then don't be afraid to do so. If your date has been hinting about moving in with them, they are obviously very serious about you. They want you to be there when they come home with open arms. At times you'll find someone who seems perfect for you, but you won't settle for them because it is not the right time. You feel that you need to see other people before finally giving in. Would you spend a lifetime looking for a mountain of gold or a week looking for a piece of copper? Learning to have fun again is very important. If you are an older man or woman who tends to take life seriously and is all about working, you probably don't have much fun. Do yourself a favor by loosening up! Show your date that you can be a fun person to be around.

The two of you can go play a fun sports game to get your blood pumping and creating positive energy. You'd be surprised at how many endorphins it let's off, leaving you with less stress. The two of you will be able to laugh and have a good time with one another. Now, if you are someone who enjoys the nightlife - why not get a margarita and go dancing with that special someone? The hint here is we only said one margarita. We don't recommend getting wasted because this will obviously ruin the date and we don't want that. Having fun means letting your guard down and being yourself. You don't have to worry about the other person judging you. The two of you can enjoy the company of one another, telling jokes, stories, and making memories together. You wouldn't act the way you act at work on a date. This is way too formal and you certainly won't get any positive response from your date. In fact, they may even find you boring and "cold". This will scare anyone away so be sure to practice being positive and having fun. Now, having fun doesn't mean going out and drinking a whole bottle of wine while dining out with your new date. You shouldn't go bar hopping either. A first date should be some place that is quiet like at a restaurant. If you are looking to save money while dating and date at least two people each week - it is a good idea to go to restaurants that aren't too expensive. Depending on your location, most items on the menu will cost $8 to $12.

Many of the restaurants will show their prices online with a detailed menu so be sure to check it out. An alternative to saving money while dating is going to an all you can eat buffet. This is great for a first time date. Besides, if you are the one paying - you never know how much your date is going to pile up on their plate! To have a little fun, you could go on a date that includes an activity. This could be something like playing volley ball, golf, or going to a body paint shop. If it is a first date, you can paint your date's face green or give them a little costume makeover. You could also give them a painted face that looks like a cheetah. This is a fun activity for the two of you and in no time, you'll both be laughing at the creations you made. Another idea would be to go to a theme park. If you are an older person who is not fond of rides, you can always visit the flower show with your date or try winning a game at a booth. Do both of you like animals? If so, another idea would be to visit the livestock or the horse race. This is a wonderful way to get to know each other and usually animals will make us feel at ease. There are plenty of benefits when it comes to mature dates. A mature person is someone who has been through just about anything in life and tends to take everything in a "casual" manner. If you tell them a dirty joke, they won't even flinch. A mature date is someone who you can rely on, trust, and have a good time with.

Most people confuse the "word" mature with being serious or even boring. A mature human is a person that is "ripe" and has experienced every season possible. They've been through so much that they won't even be alarmed if you come to the restaurant wearing a black/white cowboy hat with a pink shirt and green pants. At most, they'll probably chuckle to themselves, trying not to let you see. Mature dates come from different age groups but the average is anywhere from thirty to forty-nine years of age. If you are a mature person who is looking for someone who has the same mind set as you, you can find out by asking them certain questions. A date is similar to an interview in many cases. Naturally, you'll want to inquire about their pet peeves, what they enjoy, and even their favorite foods. One benefit of a mature date is that they ask questions about you. Because of this, you feel extremely important to them. Since they want to know information, it is a good chance they are interested. Make sure you meet them with the same level of interest. You can do this by looking into their eyes, asking them a question every now and then, or showing off certain qualities in yourself. Let your date know that you are someone who takes the relationship seriously and expect the same from them. By doing this, they'll meet you with respect and dignity. You no longer have to worry about anyone running you down again.

Push the people out of your life who aren't as mature as you are. It will save you a lot of time and stress. The best thing about dating someone mature is that they've experienced a lot in their life. Most likely, they have gone through many types of relationship issues, health problems, and by now they know how to effectively handle issues at the work place. Older men and women tend to be more calm when it comes to dating. Many of them feel inclined to rush things because they feel that they are in the middle of their life. Also, seeing friends have kids and get married is not easy either. Like we discussed before - it is not a good idea to settle down while dating. First, you need to look for that diamond in the rough. Finding that special person who makes you happy is what makes dating worthwhile. Someone who has a calm and casual attitude while dating will make you feel at ease. If you are an older mature adult and you think dating is out of the picture for you, think again! In today's day and age you do not even need to leave the house in order to meet new people. There is no point in continuing life lonely. Everyone desires a significant other and we all deserve one. Use the tips you read above and you are sure to have success in the dating game. Begin to have fun with your life and share your experiences with someone else.

It has been theorized too many times that men and women are diametrically opposite beings. The theory goes on to say that there are totally different things that drive both these genders, and there are different things that they are looking for. That is the reason men and women act and behave in radically different ways. Now, while the truth is that nature itself has ordained us to be different, which means our behaviors are characteristic of the gender that we belong to, it is also a sordid fact that this can create a lot of problems. There are several instances in which men and women do not understand each other, due to which there are disagreements and arguments between the two, even leading to drastic steps such as breakups and divorce. There are some pretty heavy and deplorable numbers about relationships that have not worked out, while it is true that if just a little more effort and understanding were used, these relationships could have worked amazingly well. We need to understand that there are different things that we look for in life, and even in a relationship, there are different things that a man and a woman look for in each other. If this one fundamental law of nature is kept in mind, then both genders would be able to live in better harmony with each other. Realizing our differences, we would be in better stead to become a unified whole. It takes time and it takes effort, but, most importantly, it takes a great deal of maturity and understanding. If we accept these differences in our partners, will have more meaningful relationships.

Very few people may be totally happy with their lives today. Surely, most lives today are shrouded by problems such as distrust among the partners, disagreements over slight issues, suspicions, ill will and even hatred. Relationships are continually souring all around us, and most times, we feel that nothing can be done about it. We resign ourselves by saying that it was meant to be that way. The shapes our relationships are taking right now are downright deplorable. 1 in 2 couples are ending up in a breakup or a divorce. The levels of animosity are definitely rising, and this is certainly no good. Why is this happening? What is it that we are failing to see? Despite making a diehard commitment at the start of our relationship, in the heydays as you may call them, what happens that makes the relationship so drastically irreparable? Certainly, the problem lies in one of the partners or both. There are some very basic things that we are completely missing out on. We are not spending the time to realize that men and women are totally different kinds of beings, and that the only way to live successfully in harmony is by understanding each other completely. If you think that is too difficult to achieve, you need to think again. You need to see that the situation is not all that bleak as it seems. There is just one link in this chain, one single strand, that we are missing out on. If we simply see this one missing link and accept it, we will be able to do much better with our lives.

That is what it is all about mutual understanding and acceptance. That is what we need to learn. And, yes, in this chapter, we begin creating the journal of your relationships that will help save your rocking relationship boat. This is your reference point and your guide, the place where you find your fumbling relationship begin to take root once again. Why is all this happening? Ultimately, it is our perceptions of what makes a good relationship and our expectations of our partner, which creates the friction in marriage. As we learn to understand why we have these expectations and how to challenge with them, we can look at our relationships with new eyes and appreciate them for what they are, rather than for what they are not, With this knowledge, all relationships potentially can move forward. Our ability to relate to each other has evolved over our lifetime. We learn by observing the culture we grew up in and through our life experiences. As children, we watch our parents and we see how they relate with each other. We interact with our siblings and this contributes to our knowledge of how people in close relationships interact with each other. We learn from talking to our friends and often compare and contrast their experiences with our own. As we reflect on what shapes the way we interact with others and why it does this, we find the key to beginning the restoration of a successful relationship.

Chapter Sixteen: Compromises

Life was completely different in the good old times, at least on the face of it. We weren't so technologically advanced back then and maybe we gave more importance to our human relationships than we do today. Man needed woman and woman needed man more than they do today that is a fact. But times have changed. We have become more mechanical, more materialistic. Our lives aren't as simple as they were before. Our obligations of the day aren't divided simply into work-time and family-time. Many more things vie for our attention each day. Still, the basic rules that were established back then are still quite prevalent. Gender roles were assigned to man and woman back then, all those centuries ago, and they still remain. Woman lib regardless. there are still gender roles that are prevalent. And this is more commonly seen when people are in a relationship. Until recently, humans traditionally mated for life with one and sometimes in polygamous societies a number of mates. Fifty years ago when people divorced, they often faced accusations and lost lifelong friendships. Today, it is likely that many of those in our circle of friends are divorced and may even have remarried with new partners. If we look back even further to the days when our ancestors were hunters and gatherers, we see a completely different situation than what is the reality for most couples today. History has shown us that our ancestors were a mainly hunting and gathering society. Men would go and hunt for food while women collected mainly seeds and berries around their home.

They relied on each other for the provision of everything material, but for the most part, they did not receive a lot of direct emotional support from each other. Instead, men developed camaraderie with the men they hunted with, while the women spent most of the time with each other, helping look after children and prepare the food. Women usually found the emotional support they needed with the women they worked with each day. This pattern continued until the 20th century. Although the type of work that men and women undertook changed drastically, the gender roles remained much the same. The man would go out to work and the woman would stay at home. This scenario is not only typically true of a western culture; studies of most world cultures reveal similar trends. Compromises hardly take relationships in the right direction. Most people who live with each other today are resigning themselves to what we call as the uneasy truce. They see the shortcomings in themselves and in their partners but keep procrastinating it until it becomes too late. They keep telling themselves that things will work out, but that never happens too soon. Are you living with this uneasy truce as well? If you are, then you should know that it is not everlasting. You are going to succumb sometime or the other, and everything is going to be in jeopardy when that happens. You may even lose out on a relationship that could have been worked out.

If there is any compromise in your relationship, you have to do something about it. You cannot stay in denial forever. You need to take stock of the situation and work in such a way that your partner as well as you are contented. Let us face it; most couples really are committed to making their relationship work. For most couples, this means pushing back the irritations and the consequences of gender differences and our feelings about them, and getting on with life as best we can. Yet, we look at others and here stories of relationships that are going well and maybe we cannot help but feel a little jealous. We keep hoping things will get better. For couples in this situation, this uneasy truce does not last forever. Eventually the pressure builds and the volcano must erupt sadly most of us are probably aware of couples we know who we thought had a happy marriage who suddenly announce they are getting divorced. Stored tension may be released in the ugliness of a bad divorce. Marriage and relationships need not be like this. A major reason why a once happy relationship reaches this point is often due to unrealized expectations by the partners in the relationship. When a couple seeks counseling, both members will express their frustration that they are doing all they can to improve the relationship. How then can an uneasy truce become a win–win situation for each member of a couple? Is it possible? Yes it is. There are a number of things that a couple can do to improve their communication and to express their feelings, in a way they know is valued, understood and appreciated by their partner.

You can take some practical steps if your relationship has reached this point to move towards a win-win situation. As you and your partner learn to appreciate how to express love and gratitude, in such a way the other partner appreciates, the relationship can start to heal. There is solid biological evidence in what we say the difference between man and woman is not just a matter of conjecture; there is an actual hormonal reason for it. While men are driven by the robust testosterone hormone a hormone that creates a kind of an aggressive edge women are governed by the milder oxytocin hormone, which compels them to give and receive love and care. So, it is not just a superficial difference that the two sexes on this planet have. There is much more. The difference runs deep inside; it deals with the hormonal composition of the two genders. That's what makes us to different. If we want to survive on this planet, we will hardly be able to do it by living in isolation and thinking about our own selfish interests. When two people in a relationship are under stress, little things often become major issues. Situations that at one stage would have been perhaps overlooked are now added to the list of things that the partner is doing wrong. Once a relationship reaches this point, it is very difficult for one or both partners to see the good things their partner can offer them and the relationship.

Men and women are driven by their hormones. Testosterone the male sex hormone, and oxytocin, the female sex hormone each play extremely important roles in the way men and women act and react. Testosterone plants a desire in men to protect and provide for their wives. Oxytocin produces a strong need in women to nurture and care for others. Adequate levels of both hormones are essential to produce a feeling of wellbeing and contentment. When both partners have high hormonal levels, they deal with life and their relationships in a positive way. When the hormonal levels are diminished, stress levels are raised, leading to greater risk of conflict within the relationship. When couples had defined roles, it was easy for the couple to live their lives with these hormones operating naturally. The man in the relationship would go to work and earn enough money to sustain his family with a suitable lifestyle and all their needs. The woman in the relationship would stay home and care for her family. When couples are in a good relationship and understanding and responding to each other's needs physically, emotionally and socially, these hormones are produced in increasing quantities. Society and circumstances has change the way we do things. Often, the man is no longer the sole provider and his wife may have a job, and yet still feel the need to nurture and care for her family.

Both of these situations create tension. The man no longer feels his wife has the same need for his provision, something that would drive him to succeed in the past. The woman feels frustrated she still often has to go home and do much of the work around the house because her husband seems to prefer to go home and sit and read the newspaper or watch the television. Testosterone and oxytocin are produced differently in each partner and once couples understand this, it will help change the way they view this scenario. In this scenario, each member of the couple is instinctively doing what is necessary for them to restore their hormonal levels. At the end of the day, both have returned home with depleted hormonal levels. To raise her levels the woman needs to nurture and care, and give and receive love to stimulate oxytocin production. Relaxation is his way of increasing his hormonal levels. The line of difference between a person who takes care of his or her own self and a person who is selfish is quite thin, but it certainly exists. As humans, we have to take care of ourselves… that is a natural tendency. Even animals do that to a lesser extent. After all, if we do not take care of ourselves, then who will? Sadly, this fact is completely misconstrued by people who are in a relationship. When a relationship begins, there is a strong likelihood of possessiveness creeping in.

Chapter Seventeen: Self Care

Along with that, there is a feeling of exaggerated self-importance. Both men and women in a relationship will expect their partners to give them more attention. Such a need for attention-showering, however, leads to several problems. It is on account of this insecurity that people in a relationship think that they are ignored when their partners are actually just taking care of themselves. We need to understand this difference. If your partner is thinking about self-care, then it is not because their love for you has dried out; it is not because they do not care about you. You can care for yourself and people with you at the same time. Maybe they are just taking care of themselves for your sake. For instance, women know that men like their women to look good. Hence, if a woman tries to look good, it might be because she wants her partner to like her. In the same coin, men who take too much care of their health may be doing so to be a better asset for their families. If a man spends money for a gym when there is shortage of money in the house, it might be because they want to stay fit in order to work and earn some more. This difference needs to be understood. To reinforce a fact that we stated earlier, both men and women are made differently. They have different desires and wishes. Hence, you need to understand that caring for oneself could have different meanings for different people. If your partner is caring for himself or herself, you should not jump to the conclusion that they are selfish.

During the time our ancestors were hunters and gatherers, and even more recently as the interiors of many of the industrialized countries were beings settled, men would go away often for days at a time and women would be at home caring for the home. During those times, men would gain the emotional support they needed with the men they travelled or worked with, and women would find the emotional support with other women. Today, there is a growing expectation that the couple will provide each other with their main supply of emotional support. Women in particular may feel quite guilty if they seek ways to have their emotional tank filled up by others or other things other than their family. Those in successful relationships do not see their partner as their main source of emotional support. Instead, their partner may only provide them with a top up supply of emotional energy, the rest is provided by self-care activities like spending time with friends or doing things that are particularly enjoyed, with or without the partner. Dropping the expectation that your partner will provide you with emotional support release them to be themselves. This will greatly influence the relationship. It reduces the need for your partner to feel they have to be perfect or act perfectly in order to please you. No one can be perfect all the time, and allowing yourself to be yourself and do the things that you enjoy doing and being around other people besides your partner will enhance the relationship.

This self-care and looking after our own emotional needs rather than putting an unnecessary burden on someone else, actually has the opposite effect to what most people imagine. Hormones are raised by these feel good activities. This creates a mutual desire to be with your partner and to share intimacy with them. The increased hormonal levels create feelings of contentment with the relationship and appreciation for the relationship. It becomes so much easier for each partner to help the other feel good about themselves and the relationship, when neither feels that that the relationship is dependent on them giving all the time. Coming together can be a celebration of what you share together. It is essential that neither member of the couple have expectations that their partner will act just like them. The differences in what makes a man a man and a woman a woman are so real, it is both unfair and completely unreasonable to expect your partner to think and act as you do in a situation. Spending time with others of your own gender enables you to talk as male-to-male or female to female in appropriate ways. This is not to devalue the need for communication between you and your partner; it just takes the pressure away from the expectations that often drive our relationships apart. One of the most important things that both partners have to remember in a souring relationship is that there is always tomorrow. Things can always be worked out for the better.

Think about it during this breach in your relationship, is it actually the fault of your partner? Are you angry with your partner or are you angry about the circumstances that forced your partner to act in a particular way? Usually, it is the latter that happens, and the people involved have to bear the brunt of a divorce or a breakup. All relationships start out well, even if they sour later on. The very fact that the relationship started out well that the two people were immensely in love with each other at the start means that things can be still worked out. Love can return. Some effort will be needed, but it is not something that cannot be accomplished at all. You need to stay optimistic; there is always a tomorrow. When you find the kinks starting in your relationship, you have to remember all that we have said before about men and women being from totally different places, and about their behavioral patterns and lists of expectations being totally different from one another. It is because of this fact that these people develop problems between them sometimes, problems that they might not be able to resolve immediately. But, most times, it only takes a good realization of the differences between them to see that it is not actually a mistake that the partner has committed, but it is just a behavioral trait within them. When you accept that fact, most of the problems will just die out.

Remember that relationships are one of the most beautiful things that Providence has created for us. We should not bring a breach in our relationship, but we must try to repair whatever problems might come our way. That is the guideline to live well, in harmony and togetherness with each other. The wonderful things about relationships are that they can always be turned around if both partners are committed to making it work. No matter how the situation in your marriage may look today, things can improve and your relationship can become a strong and lasting union. Once you have dealt with what is causing your relationship to break down, take positive steps to identify ways you can improve it. Chronic stress is a significant factor in relationship breakdown, and addressing the cause of the stress in either or both partners will immediately remove a great deal of pressure from the relationship. Whatever the cause of the stress, work as a couple to reduce it. Revise the hormonal and physiological differences between men and women and reduce the expectations you may have of marriage. This may require you and your partner to spend time reflecting on where your relationship was at the beginning, what you expected to get from your relationship, and why that expectation is not being met. Spend time reflecting on the frustrations you feel in the relationship as it is today and how you can both address these frustrations to help eliminate them.

Remember you can only change yourself not the other person. It is often easier in a painful situation, particularly one that has a lot of conflict in it, to look to blame the other partner for the problems. Instead, try perhaps with the help of friend or counselor, to look at how you can change what you are doing and modify your expectations, as you focus on gender differences and self-care to look after your own emotional needs. As a couple, determine how each of you can help support the other and provide the needs that the other partner has of you in the relationship. Women yearn to be romanced, loved and cared for. When this is a reality for her, her oxytocin levels will soar and her natural feminity will be expressed to its fullest in her. Men yearn to protect and care for their women and family members and doing this creates a peak in their testosterone levels. Relationship healing needs to include an introspective approach to how best to help your partner have these deepest needs satisfied. Although there are gender differences, it is essential that both partners understand these differences so that they can understand their partner's actions and not take them personally. Most issues in a relationship are so common that the fatal error of many a couple is to assume they are the only ones experiencing these difficulties. Plan a special day alone together or better still, plan a vacation with your partner and together discuss all the points raised in this chapter.

Together discuss the history of your relationship and honestly seek to identify common issues that are creating the problems in your relationship, especially those based on false expectations of the other partner or of the relationship. Together, plan realistic expectations of where you would like the relationship. Undeniably, the power of love is something that makes the world go around. Enmities can show power in a very cruel display that harms everyone involved and benefits no one, but love conquers all. Love can disarm people, it can make obstinate people change their minds, it can even help people with absolutely no hope to survive and look optimistically at the future. While the power of hatred is destructive, the power of love is constructive, and that is the reason why love supersedes hatred by a humongous margin. If you are in a relationship, you are already experiencing love. You are seeing how love has given a whole new meaning to your life, and now you find life more worth living. Then, why is it that so many people do not care for the love they have in their lives and make way for hatred? These are the ignorant people, the people who are not blessed with the intellect that it is love that conquers everything in the end. Even if you are faced with hatred, you have to keep in mind that it is love that you will ultimately need it is love that will sail the boat of your life. We would only like to say that the love you fostered in your relationship must be kept alive at all costs. Do not let it flicker out and die.

Take care of your partner, and understand that they are an individual in their own right too, with their own unique feelings, emotions and desires. When you entrench this single fact firmly in your mind, you find that the power of love encompasses all. In this roller coaster world of love and relationships, it is reassuring to know that fairy tale love can and does exist. Realistic expectations of love, provide an understanding that love that is deep and realistic allows the partner to make a mistake. It allows there to be inevitable differences of opinions and preferences between the couples. Anything less than this respect for the other is not true love at all. There is a saying in most philosophies that states, love covers a multitude of sins‖ This is the potential of a relationship that is based on mutual understanding and respect. In this type of relationship, a couple can appreciate and express the strengths and abilities their partner can offer them within the relationship. Negativity is replaced by positivity and even the small things that are done by the partner in a spirit of love and cooperation is accepted as an expression of that love. In this relationship, each partner is free to be them self and never feels that they need to change for the sake of the partner. The person they were at the beginning of the relationship is the person they are allowed to be at this point of the relationship. Circumstances might change, but character rarely changes.

If your relationship needs a kick-start, allow yourselves to create an adventure out of your relationship and do not let it become stale. Take time to plan to create ways to keep the excitement strong between you. Add a spark to the relationship both intimately and in other ways to create anticipation between each other. Celebrate your differences by helping each other reach your potential independently of the other and allow yourself to feel pride at the achievement of your partner. Nurture these feelings and allow yourself to express them in ways that you know your partner will recognize as your way of expressing love and appreciation to them. Don't neglect intimacy. Intimacy enables a woman to feel loved and a man to have his deepest needs met. Without a focus on intimacy, no relationship will be able to progress. Actively remember the things you used to do at the beginning of your relationship that created a surge in hormone production and actively seek to recreate those moments and add new experiences to them. Celebrate the things that make you different from your partner rather than complain about them. Develop the attitude together that your relationship is not ever going to stagnate, but that it must evolve. Life circumstances and different environments will create different stresses on the relationship, but by recognizing that you will both react differently to these pressures, you are able to support each other through them, rather than see them as a potential threat to the relationship.

Embrace your diversity and enjoy it. This is the key to a strong committed relationship. Men and women were ordained to be different by nature, and it is because of this reason that they behave in radically different ways and sometimes hurt each other. In most cases, this hurt is not intentional. A man may behave in a particular way because his behavior may dictate him to do so, but his wife may construe it as a lack of attention on his part. A woman may spend too much time looking after her beauty or after her kids, while her husband may think that she has ceased to care for him. However, in both these scenarios, we are expecting our partners to behave like us. Men expect women to behave like them, and women expect men to behave like them. This, of course, does not work. Men and women are entirely different they are hormonally different and hence they will not act like their partners. People who accept this fact find that their lives become more meaningful. They start understanding the true meaning and intention behind their partners' actions and hence they are able to put things into a better perspective. What might have culminated into an ugly war is nipped in the bud and just helps in consolidating their relationship. Relationships are a lot more than just expecting our partners to behave like us. These are the banalities of a relationship; they must be ignored as soon as possible.

Chapter Eighteen: Mind And Body

What you must look at is the larger picture whatever the differences between you, your partner has agreed to be with you for life. You have exchanged or are intending to exchange your nuptial vows in which you promise to be with them for good and for bad, in sickness and in health, till death do you part. Should these vows be dealt with so abysmally then? We need to see our relationships in new light. We have to understand that we need them to live. Our lives are enhanced only when we have love in our lives. I question how many individuals ever investigate their own inner self to think about what it is inside us that drives the demand to look externally from us and to other people for their help. When you take the time to mull over this question, I'm convinced you'll identify a principle that sounds like the following: "I no more have complete control over my own brain and body." As if you did, you wouldn't find it essential to look for outside help instead of count on your own inside capacity to help yourself. A technical enhancement for the mind would beyond any doubt be the most influential piece of equipment to own. Your mind controls so many different pieces of your life; among those is your immunity system responsible for the status of your health. Your brain likewise manages your pattern of rest and wakefulness, whether you'll arise at a particular time and if you'll have the energy to make it through your every day activities. It regulates your memory and insightfulness those factors that determine how you'll learn and remember.

You are the commander in chief of your life. There are no ifs, ands, or buts about it. You are able to attempt to give your power away and pretend to be weak, but the undeniable reality is that you're still in charge. Connect with what's most crucial to you in life. If you felt responsible for the whole world, what would you wish to change first? If you chose to become an authority at something, what would that be? What may you say about the great spirit that lies inside you, waiting for the chance to express itself through purposeful action? What truly matters to you? Even as you learn to embrace your command, you'll still come across situations where lining up with reality and might isn't adequate. In order to successfully navigate such spots, you'll have to call upon what follow in the course. In order to be able to ensure the relationship has a better chance of survival; both parties should question their roles and perceptions linked to the relationship. You should discuss compatibility, understanding, cooperation, similar hobbies, types of interests, points of disagreements and joy and any other elements that would dictate the kind of participation either party will extend towards the relationship. When it comes to the negative aspect within the relationship, both parties should be acutely aware of how these situations are tackled and the duration the negativity is present until there is some resolution in sight. There will also be a need to examine how these resolutions are sought and incorporated for the aim of getting the relationship back on track.

Making an effort to spend time together is very important if the couple intends to grow the relationship and to keep it happy and healthy for a long time to come. Without the effort to spend quality time together, the couple may find themselves eventually drifting apart and this may even lead to the eventual possibility of divorce. It is especially important to make time for each other, especially if both parties live very active and hectic professional lives. When this happens, it becomes very easy to use work and other distractions as an excuse to not make time for each other. This or course is a very bad habit to have surface during a relationship. The following are some recommendations on how to create the ideal platform for spending quality time together to keep the relationship current and strong. In the initial stages of the new relationship, these two activities are very much indulged in and even expected. However, sadly, as the relationship progresses to a more familiar phase, both parties may start taking each other for granted and one of the most popular ways of the perception becoming evident within the relationship is the lack of love letters and date nights. Most people make the mistake of thinking that such indulgences are no longer needed or necessary, thus falling into the rather boring routine that will eventually lead to the relationship getting into troubled waters. Couples who fail to continue these activates as the relationship progresses, risk being taken for granted, and when outside opportunities present themselves, there is always the possibility of being tempted to indulge in these temptations as they will find ways to justify such indulgences.

Therefore, in the quest to not only keep the relationship as exciting as first perceived, the couple should continue the exchange of love letters and date nights to also ensure there are no temptations to seek such activities elsewhere. Being active in the activities will also allow the couple to look forward to these endearing times and also ensure both parties are constantly committed to putting their "best foot forward" at all times. This would include both the physical and mental aspects within the relationship. People don't seem to understand the importance of keeping up on both these fronts. Neither party will be interested in coming home to a relationship where there is no effort put into keeping each other excited and guessing. Boredom will usually be the result of such disinterest and this will eventually force both parties to seek excitement outside the existing relationship. There is always the danger of the stay at home partner being the one that eventually allows the mental and physical appearance to go downhill. Some people just don't seem to understand the impact made on each other when there is a total lack of interest in the general upkeep, both mentally and physically. This is especially so when there are so many temptations outside the marriage perimeter, this often reminds the straying party of exactly what they are missing out on. This is often also one of the main reasons why there is infidelity and discord within a relationship that has been in existence for quite some time.

Busy schedules and commitments are often the excuses given for the lack of focus on keeping oneself in the best of conditions, both mentally and physically. If both parties don't make a concerted effort to look good for each other, it certainly gives the impression of not valuing the relationship enough. Making a spouse feel important and loved in a relationship will definitely benefit both parties as the effort made will not go unnoticed for long. Making someone feel important is not only a delightful way of expressing love and respect for the person, but is also another way of cherishing the loved one. Happily married couples will almost always attest to the fact that treating each other with respect and love goes a long way in keeping the relationship strong and being able to stand the test of time. Besides the more obvious reason such as love and respect for the spouse, this treatment will also show the level of value the individual puts on the existence of the spouse within the context of the relationship. It will also be a very natural corresponding action to return from the receiving party, thus making the relationship even stronger and longer lasting. The more popular way of extending the attitude of putting the spouse foremost in thought and deed would be to always consult the spouse when important decision are to be made that would affect each other. Others may include finding ways to keep the spouse happy and contented within the relationship, by making a conscious effort to indulge in or arrange for activities that would make the spouse feel special and loved and even buying small gifts for no particular reason, except to express love.

Simple acts that don't cause a lot of work or money such as opening a door or pulling out a chair for the spouse will go a long way in making the spouse feel special and loved. Always choosing to spend quality time with the spouse whenever the opportunity presents itself is also one way of putting the spouse on the top of the list. Marriage is not something that should be taken lightly and this is even more so when there are signs within the relationship that signify some level of trouble brewing. Most people try to take the necessary steps to save the marriage before throwing in the towel or raising the white flag in defeat. Every marriage is worth saving, and it would certainly be worth the effort to try and salvage what was once something beautiful and wonderful. This is even more important of an exercise if there are children involved. There really is not a point in giving up on a marriage and wasting many years and much effort. As long as there is still love in the picture there is still a chance of fixing things. However, it is important to know when a relationship is better ended such as toxic or abusive situations. If there is still a spark there though you should definitely try some of the above tips to fix your marriage, after all some people believe you only get one shot at true love.

The element of faith allows each person to explore these ultimate questions, while going through life as best as they can. Becoming involved in a particular faith belief will also allow the individual to be well grounded in a fundamental lifestyle. This chosen faith also allows the person to have some level of moral conscience to get through their daily activities with the proper mindset and general perception of other people, thoughts, and feelings. This makes the individual a better person to be around and also to work with. However, when there are complications within a relationship due to the varied faith beliefs, this can present quite a challenge or problem for both parties. If not handled well, this could eventually be the cause of the relationship running into serious problems. Initially taking the stand of being understanding and accommodating and even adjusting accordingly to each other beliefs might seem like the ideal path to take, however studies have shown that eventually one party will feel overwhelmingly obligated to make allowances, thus leaving them feeling stressed and even resentful. There are also cases where one party eventually tries to influence others to commit to one common faith and this too can be very stressful and damaging. This would hopefully bring forth the ideal moral person who will be an asset to society and certainly a good individual to have as a partner in any relationship!